A Path To Financial
Recovery After Divorce

A Path To Financial Recovery After Divorce

Avoid Pitfalls That Snag Divorcees
& Navigate Your Way to Financial
Independence

Michael J. Jurek, Esq.

A Path To Financial Recovery After Divorce: Avoid Pitfalls That Snag Divorcees & Navigate Your Way to Financial Independence

Published by Gatekeeper Press
2167 Stringtown Rd, Suite 109
Columbus, OH 43123-2989
www.GatekeeperPress.com

The views and opinions expressed in this book are solely those of the author and do not reflect the views or opinions of Gatekeeper Press. Gatekeeper Press is not to be held responsible for and expressly disclaims responsibility of the content herein.

The interior formatting, typesetting, and editorial work for this book are entirely the product of the author. Gatekeeper Press did not participate in and is not responsible for any aspect of these elements.

ISBN (paperback): 9781662906442
eISBN: 9781662906459

Contents

INTRODUCTION

As a divorce lawyer and financial coach, I witness on a daily basis the devastating impact that divorce has on people's finances. Unfortunately, I have found that most divorcees have no plan to achieve any sort of financial recovery as they enter the next chapter of their lives. Instead, it seems that most are (understandably) focused on making it through the day, week, and month immediately before them. They spend their energy managing their emotions and the logistical issues in their post-divorce lives but neglect their financial recovery. The divorce process leaves most physically, psychologically, and often financially exhausted. This, in turn, causes divorcees to be susceptible to making the same financial mistakes made by innumerable divorcees before them.

When it comes to characterizing what lies in front of any divorcee regarding their finances, I believe that "journey" and "recovery" are appropriate descriptors. It does not matter if the divorce was finalized ten days or ten years ago; a divorce can have lasting financial consequences long after it is finalized. While the financial devastation can be the most troubling aftereffect of divorce, I believe it is the most treatable.

For years, I have searched for a book that teaches divorcees how to avoid making common financial mistakes as they move beyond the divorce and provides them with a plan to recover financially. Since I have never been able to find that book, I wrote this one. It is filled with advice and recommendations that I have long wished to bestow on all divorcees.

If you are reading this, I can only assume that you are either recovering from your divorce, or you want to help someone close to you recover from their divorce. This book is intended for both audiences.

IF YOU ARE A DIVORCEE, I know the heartbreak, sadness, loneliness, fear, and anxiety you feel because I see it in my clients' faces and hear it in their voices every day. The overwhelming majority of my clients must cope with the harsh reality of a lower household income and lingering debt obligations post-divorce. The inevitable change in lifestyle and financial hit from losing a chunk of their net worth, retirement, and possessions only adds to their uneasiness. My guess is that you can relate to some or all of this.

My goal is for you to achieve a level of prosperity that you had previously thought to be impossible, given the financial setback you have endured. This is a guidebook that is meant to help you develop and follow a plan so you can avoid making the same financial mistakes repeated by all-too-many divorcees.

Dwelling on the past and circumstances that led you here will get you nowhere. Our focus will be on the steps you need to take to gain control of your finances, eliminate the debts in your life, build up your retirement, and be in a significantly better financial position than you were the day your divorce was finalized. To take control of your finances, you have to create a budget and stick to it with a level of discipline not necessarily required of you while you were still married. Living on a budget is challenging under the best of circumstances; adhering to one while dealing with disruptions in almost all other aspects of your life makes it exponentially more difficult.

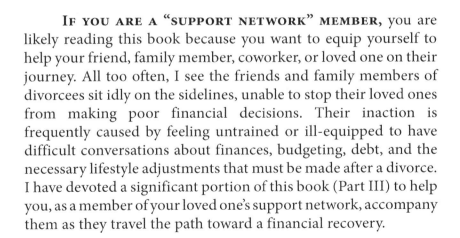

> *You can't go back and make a new start, but you can start right now and make a brand-new ending.*
> **– James R. Sherman**

Your starting point doesn't matter; you might be flush with cash or up to your eyeballs in debt, but either way, you need a plan. This book will help you formulate that plan both in your mind and on paper, and you will walk away knowing the steps you need to take to get back on the road to financial prosperity.

⬤

IF YOU ARE A "SUPPORT NETWORK" MEMBER, you are likely reading this book because you want to equip yourself to help your friend, family member, coworker, or loved one on their journey. All too often, I see the friends and family members of divorcees sit idly on the sidelines, unable to stop their loved ones from making poor financial decisions. Their inaction is frequently caused by feeling untrained or ill-equipped to have difficult conversations about finances, budgeting, debt, and the necessary lifestyle adjustments that must be made after a divorce. I have devoted a significant portion of this book (Part III) to help you, as a member of your loved one's support network, accompany them as they travel the path toward a financial recovery.

⬤

This book is divided into three parts, all of which are relevant to you regardless of whether you are a divorcee or a support network member.

PART I is devoted to exposing and dissecting the most common, destructive, and avoidable financial mistakes that divorcees consistently make and stall their recovery. I have observed these slip-ups so frequently that my initial inspiration for writing this book was to help stop my own clients from making these blunders over and over and over again. Each mistake is not only avoidable but also has the potential to set you back financially for years, if not a decade or longer. The difficulty is that all of these missteps are easy to make, and some can be made in the blink of an eye due to a moment of weakness. I will teach you to identify and avoid these damaging financial traps.

PART II lays out a roadmap for you to follow to get out of debt, build up your emergency fund, and save for retirement. You will be able to find peace when it comes to your finances when you develop and stick to a plan to achieve these goals. All of this is certainly possible for you, so long as you follow the steps spelled out in this section of the book and avoid the financial mistakes discussed in Part I. This portion of the book will also answer the ultimate question: *Where do I go from here?* It will provide you with direction and guidance for the next steps you should take in your post-divorce financial journey.

PART III is dedicated to educating and guiding those in the divorcee's support network on how to help their loved one. If you are reading this because you want to help someone near and dear to your heart, bless you. I am your biggest supporter. I have nothing but respect for anyone who volunteers to walk alongside a loved one who has been rattled by the divorce process. You have an incredibly difficult role to play because of the many different hats you will need to wear. Sometimes you will be the shoulder to cry on; other times, you will have to be the voice of reason, speaking hard truths contrary to what your loved one wants to hear. Your role requires a delicate balance, and its challenges are many. This book will guide you through the difficulties of serving in this role and empower you to be the adept wingman your loved one needs. After reading Part I, you will be able to spot the financial pitfalls that ensnare so many divorcees and help yours to avoid them. You will also be able to act as an "accountability partner" to your loved one (covered in Part II) to assist them with budgeting, spending, saving, and debt elimination. Finally, Part III of this book speaks specifically to you as the confidant and provides you with guidance, tips, and advice while serving in this vital and delicate role.[1]

There are five essential tenets for you to bear in mind as we venture ahead.

First and foremost, how you arrived at your current position is of little concern. Instead, your success going forward will be determined by what you do from this point onward. When it comes to your recovery, I do not want you to get hung up on what brought you to your current financial situation. The past is the past, and there is nothing you or I can do to change it. Our focus, from here on out, is on the future. Just like any other aspect of your life, if mistakes were made, learn from them, and try not to repeat them. If you have regrets, join the club. Just know that the only thing you can change is your behavior today and every day hereafter.

> *It isn't where you came from, it's where you're going that counts.*
> *– Ella Fitzgerald*

---

1. From this point until Part III, I am going to use the word "you" to speak directly to divorcees.

Second, since this is a book about your finances, there will be virtually no discussion about your mental health. I am not a mental health expert, so it would be irresponsible for me to venture too deep into the emotional aspect of your post-divorce recovery.[2] That said, we cannot expect to make any progress with your financial recovery if you neglect your mental health. In other words, if you fail to address your emotional needs, you are hamstringing your ability to prosper financially. How do I know this? Because retail therapy is a real thing. An impulse purchase made under the guise of retail therapy can mean more debt, can sabotage your budget, and stifle your ability to pay down other debt. Phrases such as *"I deserve this"* and *"I really don't need this, but it will make me happy"* are used every day by divorcees to justify bad financial decisions that deepen their debt and make their journey toward recovery that much more difficult. Therefore, if your sole focus is on your mental health— which includes buying things that you cannot afford so you feel temporarily happy—at the expense of your financial health, you will continue to be plagued by the stress, anxiety, and angst that comes with being broke. Conversely, when your finances are under control, you will find peace from having no debt and a stocked emergency fund.

Third, your financial recovery is not a sprint. It is instead a marathon that is going to require steady discipline over a significant length of time. Depending on your starting point, getting out of debt may take just a few months or take several years. Only when your debts are cleared will you be in

---

2. There are many available resources that are specifically designed to aid in emotional recovery after separation and divorce, including professional counselors, books, articles, support groups, and online tools. I recommend looking into Divorce Care, which is a time-tested and highly respected 13-week program that is offered at churches and community centers across the country. (Visit *DivorceCare. com* for more information). Just as you are seeking guidance with your financial recovery, I strongly encourage you to do the same for your emotional recovery.

the position to build wealth and eventually achieve financial independence. That said, the concept of *recovery* means different things to different people. You may not feel *recovered* until you hit a certain balance in your bank account or eliminate every debt you owe. Or, quite possibly, a full financial recovery may be a feeling that eludes you for a decade or more. Your journey won't be like your divorce, which had a definitive ending when the court issued the final judgment decree legally terminating your marriage. Instead, your financial recovery will be a process that will take an undetermined amount of time. There are no shortcuts or quick fixes that I can offer. How long it takes for you to complete this undertaking depends on multiple factors, including your income relative to your debt, your ability to increase that income, your spending and lifestyle, your intensity when it comes to saving and investing, and your financial goals. If you follow the guidelines outlined herein, you will see fantastic results. It will not happen overnight, but it will eventually happen if you stick to your plan.

Fourth, you may notice that your support network may be absent during this stage of your journey. You may feel that you are traveling this road alone because those who were always by your side when your divorce first started have vanished over time. From what I have observed, this is quite common. It was first brought to my attention many years ago by a former client of mine named Kelly.[3]

I saw Kelly at the grocery store several years after her divorce. She was an avid runner and a hard-working registered nurse who was generally good with her money. When I asked her how things were going, Kelly revealed the struggles she had encountered. She described her experience as something akin

---

3. To protect the privacy of my former clients, I have changed all the names in this book.

to running two marathons, back-to-back, with no break in-between and a sparse crowd of supporters to cheer her on during the second course. Kelly said:

> *The day my divorce was over, it felt like I just got done running a marathon. It was hell, and I was glad to be done with it. I was emotionally exhausted and financially drained. I knew that our finances were in terrible shape and that I would be responsible for cleaning up much of the mess Ryan and I created. Yet while I was happy the legal part was over, it felt like I had to gear up for another 26.2 miles right away— but with ankle weights, a headwind, and a course that went straight uphill. Even worse, I felt like I had to do it all alone.*

Kelly told me that she leaned on her friends, sister, parents, coworkers, and pastor during the divorce. By the time her divorce concluded nearly a year later, however, she had found that most of her supporters had become, as she described it, "disinterested" in hearing about her struggles.

Kelly's description of the collective fatigue exhibited by her support network reminded me of the phenomena that psychologists classify as compassion fatigue—something divorce lawyers are often warned about in trade publications and at continuing education seminars. Compassion fatigue is defined as "the cumulative physical, emotional, and psychological effect of exposure to traumatic stories or events when working in a helping capacity, combined with the strain and stress of everyday life."[4] Doctors, nurses, caregivers, therapists, funeral directors, and countless other professionals—who regularly attend to individuals in physical and emotional distress—are warned to

---

4. *Compassion Fatigue*, AM. BAR ASS'N, https://www.americanbar.org/groups/lawyer_assistance/resources/compassion_fatigue (last visited October 4, 2020).

look out for signs of burnout, fatigue, and indifference because the repeated exposure to stress in their occupation, when combined with the non-work stressors in their own lives, can become overwhelming.

In other words, every one of us has a finite capacity for stress; we have to handle the stressors in our own lives and thus have a limited ability to take on others' stress. In the years since my conversation with Kelly, many of my former clients have recounted similar experiences of disinterested family members and friends at later stages in their journey when those supporters were most needed. So, be aware that your friends, family members, and coworkers may, at some point, become unavailable to you because they have their own issues and challenges that consume their time.

To someone who hasn't lived through a divorce, it might seem that the most urgent times a loved one needs help are: (1) at the outset of the divorce action when coming to grips with the fact that the marriage is over, which is incredibly difficult, and (2) at various times during the litigation of the divorce action, including the days leading up to the final hearing. Few recognize that the most challenging time might instead be after the dust of the legal process has settled.

In Kelly's case, her support network vanished when she entered the next chapter of her life, which involved a significant amount of debt, a substantially lower household income, and severe emotional distress. While Kelly was forever thankful to those in her life who got her through the end of the legal process, she discovered that the second part of her journey, which involved recovering emotionally and financially after the divorce, was much more complicated than the first part. Not having the same enthusiastic group of supporters in her corner made the latter part of her journey even harder.

> *The truth will set you free, but first it will piss you off.*
>
> **– Gloria Steinem**

Fifth, I must forewarn you that we will be covering topics *very* personal to you, including your spending, your house, your car, your lifestyle, your children, your ex-spouse, your goals, and that melodramatic five-year-old alter ego inside of you. The advice in this book is not meant to be insensitive to your situation. Far from it. We must cut through all your emotions and focus on finding solutions to the problems you face for this entire endeavor to work.

In the spirit of honesty, I am not going to sugarcoat anything. I believe it is in your best interest that the topics in this book be addressed truthfully and directly. Your financial success is our paramount goal, and that cannot be achieved without acknowledging cold, hard truths. I need you—and *you* need you—to be honest about your objectives and the level of hard work, dedication, and discipline you will need to attain those goals. Contrary to that voice in your head saying, *"I'm all out of gas,"* I can assure you that you have more left in your tank. I know this because you chose to pick up this book about getting your financial affairs in order. That is an act of a person who wants to make the next year of their life better than the one before. Regardless of your goals—breaking free of a paycheck to paycheck servitude; sleeping soundly at night without any worries about your finances; paying for your child's college education; or saving enough money so you can retire with dignity—you are reading this because you want to improve your financial situation. You have come to the right place.

You can accomplish everything laid out in the pages ahead by avoiding the mistakes that regularly hamper other divorcees and take the steps necessary to gain total control of your finances. Achieving success with your money is going to take hard work, sacrifice, and dedication. But you can do it. This book is going to show you how.

Let's get to work.

PART I:

FINANCIAL MISTAKES DIVORCEES COMMONLY MAKE AND HOW TO AVOID THEM

Since I encounter divorcees who have made the mistakes outlined in this section so frequently, I felt a need to write this book to help others save their money, sanity, and time. If you can learn from others' mistakes, you will be in the best position possible to succeed on your journey toward financial recovery.

> *It's good to learn from your mistakes.*
> *It's better to learn from other people's mistakes.*
>
> **– Warren Buffett**

MISTAKE #1:

TRYING TO MAINTAIN THE SAME LIFESTYLE YOU LIVED DURING THE MARRIAGE

There is no escaping that your household income post-divorce is lower than when you were married. This means your lifestyle must change. Depending on the magnitude of the hit to your income, you may need to sell your house, downgrade to a less expensive car, skip vacations and restaurant visits until you are debt-free, give up pricey memberships and subscriptions, change your cell phone plan, cut cable, alter your shopping habits, and forgo both big and small luxuries in your life. It also means that, more than ever before, you must get on a budget and stick to it.

You cannot continue to live the same lifestyle you enjoyed during the marriage.

You may find yourself deep in debt and owing money to everyone under the sun, including credit card companies, auto lenders, family members, friends, and even your divorce attorney. Even more infuriating is that you may be responsible for paying off debt that your ex-spouse incurred, despite your objections to them taking on that debt in the first place. It's also quite possible that you will be left holding the bag for a debt that you didn't even know existed until the divorce proceedings because your former partner hid it from you during the marriage. None of that changes the math.

To get out of debt, you must live below your means to have money available at the end of every month to pay extra on your debts until they are extinguished. Before your divorce, your household had a more considerable top-line income that gave you latitude in your spending. Even if your spouse stayed at home while you were the sole breadwinner, they still handled tasks like childcare, cooking, cleaning, laundry, ironing, and grocery shopping that will now cost you time and money to replace.

You may be thinking that "live below your means" is an obvious platitude and hardly profound advice. However, it is the mantra that has been practiced for generations by grandmas and millionaires alike—because it works. It is a mindset and way of living that you have no choice but to adopt. Going from two incomes down to one means all of your expenses—including the modest, frequent, and non-essential purchases that chip away at the money in your wallet—are now subject to scrutiny.

At this point, you must reassess your spending and formulate a budget based upon your new household income. While budgeting will be discussed in-depth in Part II of this book, the reason I mention it here is that when you sit down to create your first budget, your lifestyle cannot be stuck in the past. Simply put, your goal cannot be to maintain the lifestyle you enjoyed during the marriage. The longer you try to live the way you used to, the longer it will take you to see any financial progress because you are living above your means. It is axiomatic that with a lower household income, your budget is going to be tighter. That means some, if not many, things in your life must change.

Start by categorizing your spending as *wants* and *needs*. For example, your housing is a *need*, whereas the newest iPhone is a *want*, despite convincing yourself that you simply *must* have it. Believe it or not, a sizable portion of your expenditures are on *wants* and not *needs*. Since you face a dramatic decrease in household income post-divorce, a close examination of your *wants* versus your *needs* is a necessary and eye-opening part of this process. You will probably be surprised by how much money you spend every month on *wants*, not *needs*, and how these *wants* can keep you in a financial hole.

Let's start small. Consider some of the everyday expenses that can act as ankle weights during your journey.

Start by examining those small, almost-daily, recurring purchases.

1. Your daily "vice" can cost you serious coin.

I'll preface this by saying that I readily acknowledge that one of the most cliché pieces of financial advice out there is to *cut out your daily Starbucks habit.* I get it—not everyone goes to Starbucks every day, but Starbucks became a household name synonymous with expensive coffee because millions of people do.[5]

Nevertheless, the cliché advice, in all honesty, is not all wrong because, for most people, there is a daily or almost-daily regular expense in your life that you could eliminate to save a significant sum of money. The basic message is lost, though, because it is so oft-repeated with a *pull yourself up by your bootstraps* tone of condescension.

That said, to take control of your finances, you need to look at your spending habits—and that analysis must start with the small, basic, and often daily expenditures. The person who frivolously spends $2,400 on one big purchase a year is no different than the person who frivolously spends $200 a month (or $46 per week) on regular, unnecessary purchases. The easiest place to begin is to look at where you spend your money most days in a given week. It may not be Starbucks for you but instead some other recurrent "vice" that slowly but surely drains your bank account a few bucks at a time.

Coffee, cigarettes, alcohol, fast food, and the daily snack purchased at the convenience store are common culprits because they all add up over time. In particular, coffee drinkers and Starbucks happen to take the most heat from personal finance authors; eliminating one's daily coffee expense is frequently touted as the panacea to fix strained budgets. These same

---

5. Starbucks consistently generates revenue that exceeds $20 billion every year, so plenty of people clearly buy their products on a regular basis. See *Starbucks Annual Reports,* available at https://www.annualreports.com/Company/starbucks-corp (last visited October 4, 2020).

authors have more recently targeted avocado toast—a trendy food option, as you know, that didn't seem to exist before 2019. Yet, the point remains the same: these regular, sometimes daily transactions will slowly and steadily bleed your bank account over the course of a year.

So, because millions of people get their daily coffee fix by stopping at Starbucks or one of its many competitors every single day, this is a good place to start. The typical everyday Starbucks customer presumably justifies their purchases by thinking: *"It's not a big deal. It's only a few bucks a day. There's no way I'm going to give up my coffee!"* But consider the cost of that daily latté, cappuccino, or sugary iced beverage when added up over a year:

$4 per day x 7 days a week   = $28 per week

$4 per day x 30 days a month   = $120 per month

$28 per week x 52 weeks a year   =   **$1,456 per year**

This math assumes the daily purchase is limited to $4 per day, tax included, and assumes one visit per day.

For the cigarette smoker, the math (if you are honest with yourself) is no different and possibly much worse. The number of packs per week you smoke multiplied by the cost per pack multiplied by 52 weeks in a year may make that Starbucks regular seem like a penny-pincher.

To my beer and wine drinkers, fast foodies, and convenience store snackers who scoff at the amount spent by smokers and coffee connoisseurs: multiply your own regular "vice" expenditure for the week by 52. Are you spending more than $1,000 per year? More than $2,000 per year?

2. Workplace lunches out + happy hours = unhappy bank account.

We all know coworkers who eat lunch out of the office or order takeout every workday. I may be describing you. On a day-to-day basis, it may not seem like much. Some days it's $6; other days, it is $13. But, hey, you need to eat lunch, right? If you spend $7.50 for lunch every day during the workweek, you will end up paying $1,875 over the entire year. You could undoubtedly brown bag it for a fraction of that cost.

$7.50 per lunch x 5 workdays a week   = $37.50 per week

$37.50/workweek x 50 workweeks a year   =   **$1,875 per year**

Lunch is just one example of a daily expenditure that can add up, and a minor one at that. Say you like to go out after work once a week for a happy hour with your friends or coworkers. Your logic might be that happy hours are an excellent way to bond with your coworkers. Plus, you might think: *"The cost of an appetizer, some drinks, and the tip once a week is not going to break the bank because it's only $20 one night a week!"*

$20 per workweek x 50 workweeks a year = **$1,000 per year**

Add the cost of a weekly happy hour to your daily lunch and vice expenses, and you are already at over $4,000 per year.

3. Restaurants can chew through your bank account.

Several years ago, I was asked to provide some financial coaching for Meredith, a recently divorced mother of two, who was referred to me by a local church. She had never lived on a budget before but was seeking my help to get her finances in order. Right at the start, Meredith informed me that in the six months since her divorce was finalized, she had been unable to save or invest anything, despite having an above-average household income from her job and child support. In other words, she was treading water. Her first homework assignment was to put together a simple beginner's budget, which involved looking at her past few months of expenses.

When Meredith arrived at our second meeting, she shared her mixed emotions. Meredith said she was happy because she had successfully created a budget that identified where all her money was going. Yet she was also angry at herself for spending so much money at restaurants during the six months that followed her divorce. Meredith realized that she was spending roughly $400 per month eating out at restaurants, despite her explanation that she and her kids "don't even eat anywhere fancy!"

Meredith described how even a fast-casual restaurant like Chipotle cost her more than $30 a visit for her and her two boys. She showed me her latest receipt, which was evidence of how costly a spur-of-the-moment restaurant visit could be for her:

3 burritos @ $7.50 each:	$22.50
3 soft drinks @ $1.70 each:	$5.10
1 order of chips & guacamole:	$3.25
Total (pre-tax):	**$30.85**

Meredith told me that the unplanned dining out occurred, on average, twice a week. She said that the decision to eat out was typically made on a whim, due to a combination of her children's activities ending late, the lack of a planned or prepared meal at home, and her exhaustion at the end of the workday. Worse yet, she said in addition to the one or two unplanned visits, she and her kids had planned outings which often took place on the weekends. When Meredith was married, the family ate out at the same frequency or slightly more, but it was not as big of a deal because there was more money thanks to the combined incomes.

Between the planned and unplanned restaurant visits and takeout orders, Meredith's $400/month trajectory put her on track to spend **$4,800 per year**, just on restaurants and takeout. Even worse, she revealed that neither she nor her ex-husband had saved *anything* for their children's college funds. Upon realizing that she was effectively *eating* the money that could put her kids through college, Meredith committed to making a change. She decided to begin budgeting $50/month ($12.50/week) for a carry-out pizza night with her children; the other $350 Meredith had been spending on dining out was now earmarked for their college funds.

Sure enough, two months later, Meredith cheerfully reported that she stuck to her plan and saved $350 for each child's college savings account, which was a major accomplishment considering that she and her now ex-husband had saved *nothing* for college during the first decade of their children's lives when their combined household income had been significantly higher.

When I followed up with Meredith nearly a year after our final appointment, she told me that she successfully cut other expenses from her budget as well. She was investing $300 in each child's college savings account. Her investment advisor projected that with an 8% annual rate of return, Meredith's older son would have roughly $33,000 saved by the time he was college-bound, and her younger son would have approximately $47,000 in his account at age 18. Meredith achieved this feat by prioritizing her spending, living on a budget, and diverting money away from restaurants and toward her children's future instead.

Now for the moment of truth: how much do *you* spend at restaurants each week? $25? $50? $100? More? Do you have any idea? Basic math shows that the annual cost of $50 per week spent on restaurants equates to $2,600 per year.

$50 per week x 52 weeks = **$2,600 per year**

Again, this assumes you are spending $50 a week. In Meredith's case, her restaurant expenditures were usually made on a whim, without any serious planning, and justified based on convenience. She came to realize that proper meal planning, a crockpot, her freezer, and even her microwave could mean the difference between her children having to take out student loans to go to college and them graduating debt-free.

4. Cut the cable. Ditch the Dish.

You may have heard about the "cut the cord" movement, which involves millions of households ditching traditional cable and satellite television packages in favor of significantly cheaper alternatives. Before high-speed internet, there were only a few ways to get content delivered to your television: cable, satellite, or an antenna. Now, content can be instantly delivered to your phone, tablet, and television through countless streaming and on-demand services, some of which offer massive catalogs (like Netflix, Hulu, and Amazon Prime) at a fraction of the cost of cable and satellite, or even at no charge (like Crackle and Vudu). If you are spending $100 per month on your cable or satellite subscription, you are not alone. Annually, though, that is a significant expense.

$100 per month x 12 months a year = **$1,200 per year**

If you still have an expensive cable or satellite package, consider cutting the cord and saving yourself a bunch of money. If you have the internet at your residence and don't have a smart TV, you can buy a device such as a Roku, Amazon Fire TV Stick,

Chromecast, or Apple TV as a substitute for traditional cable or satellite providers. These devices will allow you to stream Hulu, Amazon Prime (tens of thousands of movies and television shows are included for free if you have a Prime subscription for $12.99/month or $119/year), Netflix, or a streaming television provider such as Sling, at a significantly reduced cost compared to cable. Alternatively, your local library also has a broad and continuously updated array of movies and television series on Blu-ray or DVD that are available for you to borrow for free. Still, if you go overboard and load up on streaming subscriptions, you will not be able to recognize any savings. But if you are smart with your subscriptions and buy an amplified HD antenna so you can pick up the local stations at no charge, you can save hundreds of dollars every year and still have more programming options than you have time to watch.

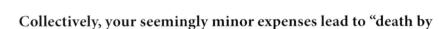

Collectively, your seemingly minor expenses lead to "death by a thousand cuts."

All of the expenses mentioned above are minor luxuries in this modern era. They are all *wants*—not *needs*—because you don't *need* any of them to survive. Add them all up, and you will be astonished at the collective impact they have not only on your wallet but on your ability to pay down debt:

Daily vice @ $4 per day	$1,460 per year
Workday lunch @ $7.50 per day	$1,875 per year
Happy Hour @ $20 per week	$1,000 per year
Restaurants @ $50 per week	$2,600 per year
Dish/cable @ $100 per month	$1,200 per year
Total:	**$8,135 per year**

According to the Bureau of Labor Statistics, in 2018, the average salary in the U.S. for 25 to 64-year-olds was approximately $47,000 per year before taxes and health insurance. Eliminating just one of the expenses we have identified would put extra dollars back in the average American's bank account. And collectively, the cost of the aforementioned expenses could easily eat up a substantial percentage of your take-home pay. Yet, with simple lifestyle changes, you can replace every single one of these luxuries at a *fraction* of the cost.

- If you are a coffee drinker, you have a coffeemaker at home. Buy a good travel mug and quit the daily stop. You'll save yourself more than $1,250 per year.

- Pack your lunch every day and skip the weekly happy hour. Between these two expenses, you can save more than $2,000 per year.

- Avoid the convenience store. Buy snacks in bulk to keep in your car to keep from having to pay convenience store prices when you're hungry. Quitting smoking will save you so much money, both in the short-term and long-term.

- How much faster could you pay off debt if you are not spending *thousands of dollars a year* on restaurants, take-out, and delivery? If convenience is an issue, setting up a crockpot before you leave for work in the morning, using a pressure cooker, or even firing up your microwave are all ways to have a meal ready in a short amount of time after a long day and at a substantial cost savings to your alternative.

- Save hundreds of dollars every year by ditching cable, dish, and whatever premium channels you

have. If you buy an amplified high-definition
TV antenna at a one-time expense of $25 and
supplement it with an $8 per month streaming
service, you can save a lot of money every month
and still will not have time to watch all of the
shows your friends and coworkers tell you that
you should watch. Just don't make the mistake of
paying for too many subscriptions and features
you do not use. Plus, your parents were right—*too
much television will rot your brain.*

These are just a handful of expenses that must be
reexamined when your household income drops significantly.
They are also just the tip of the iceberg as your spending analysis
should dive much, much deeper. Look at your bank statements,
credit card statements, and the pile of receipts scattered around
your car to see how you spent your money each month over the
past six months. Then ask yourself, for each recurring expense:
"Can I save money by eliminating or reducing this expense?"

Seriously, you should reexamine *all* of your expenses.

At the risk of sounding like a cell phone salesperson, have
you considered changing cell phone service providers? It could
save you lots of money. For every major cell phone carrier whose
commercials you cannot seem to avoid, numerous discount
sub-brand cell phone services use the same towers, provide
the same coverage, and offer more favorable terms at less cost.
Suppose you currently use AT&T, Verizon, or T-Mobile. In
that case, ten minutes of internet research on the topic will
produce a comparable sub-brand of each of those companies or
a competitor that leases network access from the major carriers.
In other words, you can get the same cell phone service on the

same network you currently use at significant savings. Why pay $85 per month when you can get the same service on the same network for $35 per month? Do the research, make the switch, keep your same number, and save hundreds per year, per phone line.

You have heard countless commercials ask: "*Are you paying too much for your auto, homeowners, or renter's insurance?*" This is a great question. When was the last time you shopped around to see if you are getting the best coverage at the best price for your home and auto insurance? If it has been a while, be sure to talk with a local insurance broker—not a captive agent who can only offer insurance through State Farm or Allstate, for example, but someone who can shop the rates of a bunch of different insurance companies. If you can save money by switching your automobile and homeowners (or renters) insurance carrier, do it. Consider raising the deductible on your automobile and homeowners (or renters) insurance if you are in the financial position to shoulder a larger share of the risk because the higher the deductible, the less your insurance will cost. Determine the level of risk you are willing to bear, and price your insurance policies accordingly.

Most communities have a mix of expensive and more economical grocery stores. Are you doing your grocery shopping at the less expensive grocery store? If you have an ALDI or Lidl in your area, be sure to pay them a visit. For your non-grocery needs, are you able to buy what you need on eBay, Craigslist, or Facebook Marketplace? Can you find a digital coupon app to clip coupons while you are sitting on the couch? Every dollar matters when you experience a significant drop in your household income, so big savings can mean a big difference in your journey.

By modifying your behavior to reduce your expenses and paying attention to where and how you spend your money, you can avoid the *death by a thousand cuts* and eliminate those unnecessary recurring expenses that heretofore have bled your wallet dry.

━━━━━●━━━━

Let's be clear: It's not just the smaller expenses that need to be scrutinized.

I intentionally started this discussion by addressing the smaller recurring expenses in your life because, frankly, it is easier to convince someone to brew their own coffee than it is to persuade them to sell their car or house. However, the reality is that curtailing the smaller expenditures, while helpful, may just be a drop in the bucket compared to your vehicle and your home.

As of March 2020, according to Edmunds, the average car payment in the U.S. was $569 per month on a loan term of 70.6 months—just shy of six years.[6] Thus, before gas, insurance, and maintenance, a $569 monthly car payment represents $6,828 a year siphoned from your take-home pay. Even worse, your car is quickly going down in value like a rock. Therefore, if you are like the average American car buyer, you will have paid roughly $40,000 for a car that, at the end of the loan, will be worth less than $10,000.

A $569 monthly car payment is an absolute killer for many single-income household budgets. If an extra $400 or $500 per month would give you breathing room in your monthly budget that you desperately need, it may be time to put your car up for sale. (*Stay tuned: Your house will be discussed in the next chapter.*)

This is not about being able to "afford" the monthly payment.

I understand the sentiment. "Affordability"—especially when it comes to car payments—is a proposition that has been

---

6. Ronald Montoya, *How Long Should a Car Loan Be?*, EDMUNDS (April 10, 2020), https://www.edmunds.com/car-loan/how-long-should-my-car-loan-be.html.

pounded into our brains for decades. You cannot watch any sort of television programming without seeing a car commercial. Despite the features of the newest and most technically-advanced vehicle being peddled, literally every car commercial ends the same way—with all of the financing promotions and lease options available to you, the presumed "well-qualified buyer." Every financing promotion is intended to convince you that you too can be driving a new car for a "reasonable" and "affordable" monthly payment.

The problem is that all of the teaser finance offers available to you on your car are also available to you for your home furnishings, mattress, appliances, home repairs, and even your day-to-day purchases. When you have monthly payments on your mortgage, car, furniture, cell phone, television, credit cards, student loans, and everything else you have financed, there may not be any money left at the end of the month for you to save, invest, and get ahead.

The best guidance I have ever found on automobile affordability comes from Dave Ramsey, a personal finance expert,[7] and host of *The Dave Ramsey Show*. Dave tells the 12 million daily listeners on his nationally-syndicated radio show to sell their car if: (1) it costs more than 50% of their household income, and (2) they cannot pay off all of their debts (excluding their mortgage but including the car) inside of 24 months. In other words, if your annual household income is $40,000, the maximum value of your vehicle (or vehicles) should not exceed $20,000. If your annual household income is $80,000, the value of your car(s) should not exceed $40,000. Someone who makes $40,000 per year should not be driving a $40,000 truck because

---

7. Dave Ramsey is a personal hero of mine. In addition to his radio show, Dave is a *New York Times* best-selling author of many books, including *The Total Money Makeover*, which has sold more than five million copies and helped guide millions of people out of debt. In Part II of this book, I advocate anyone needing to get out of debt to follow his guidance. As such, you will see his name throughout this book.

that person cannot afford to turn $40,000 into $10,000—which is what the car will eventually be worth in a matter of years. Dave consistently tells his listeners that when you have too much tied up in cars relative to your income, too much of your net worth is going down in value (as cars *always* do). Those who achieve wealth get there by putting their money in things that go up in value.

Additionally, even if someone making $60,000 has a $30,000 vehicle, if they cannot pay off the car loan *and* all of their other non-mortgage debts inside two years, they should sell the car ASAP because they will be in debt too long.

I would highly encourage you to apply this guideline to your own vehicle situation. You may realize that putting your vehicle up for sale and buying something less expensive for cash would be a game changer for your monthly budget. This will be discussed in greater detail in Part II.

If you have a hefty car payment and regular indulgences, you are robbing from your future self.

If you are still not convinced that these "drastic" changes need to be made in your life, consider the long-term implications that your car payment and the other non-essential *wants* are having on your future net worth. These monthly expenses are not only depriving you of your ability to pay off debt but also your ability to invest money in your children's college funds, save for your retirement, and pay off your home mortgage.

If you were to save and invest $750 per month (which can quickly be done by eliminating a monthly $569 car payment and another $200 per month you are otherwise spending on restaurants, bars, cable, cell phones, daily vices, etc.) for 25 years—say from age 40 to 65—at an 8% rate of return you would have more than $700,000. This figure does not even include your retirement savings or any other investing you do along the way. It can be generated by simply not spending all your money on things that chip away at your budget every month and instead investing it in your future.

Would your life be drastically different if you made your coffee at home, packed all of your lunches, completely cut out bars and restaurants until you were debt-free, cut the cable/dish subscription, switched your cell phone plan, and had no car payment because you drove around in a paid-for vehicle? No, probably not. You may try to convince yourself otherwise, but my job is to point out that you can handle all of these changes, especially if these "sacrifices" only last a limited amount of time.

One of the many worries my clients face is the fear of losing their identity post-divorce. While married, they may have been able to spend money without thinking, travel the world, drive an expensive car, and live in a luxurious house. Though, living a particular lifestyle and buying high-priced things does not define anyone, nor does it make up their personality. You may be thinking: "*If I can't afford to go to the same gym, go out for coffee and dinners with my friends, and have to turn down happy hours and drinks with my coworkers, I'm going to lose my friends!*" If so, I encourage you to find other ways to maintain those friendships that do not set you back financially. If your friendship with someone is so weak that it cannot survive without you spending money to be in their company, I question if that person is truly a friend. If they're aware you are recovering from a divorce—and thus have recently seen a significant drop in your household income—they shouldn't hold your inability to attend an expensive show or eat at a pricey restaurant against you.

Nonetheless, it is important for you to realize that your friends and acquaintances may not understand how your financial situation has changed, the depth of the debt you are facing, or the hit to your household income. While you may want to keep the specifics of your finances to yourself, it is up to you to speak up when a friend asks you to do something you cannot afford. Don't let yourself be peer pressured into busting your budget, even if it is done $10 and $20 at a time. Instead of feeling pressured into accepting an invitation to do something that is not in your budget, such as regularly going out to restaurants or bars, respond by inviting them to your residence for coffee or drinks instead. Or, if the weather is nice, bring a thermos and suggest going for a walk in the park. If they ask you to go out to a meal at a restaurant, you may need to politely decline by saying, *"it's not in my budget this month, but if you want to bring over an appetizer and dessert, I'll make the main dish."*

The same methodology is effective with coworkers. If you eat your packed lunch every day in the lunchroom, others may follow suit. The simple phrase *"it's not in my budget"* is the perfect excuse in any situation where you may feel pressured to spend money you cannot spare. This lets the person extending the invitation know that you are not declining because of them; rather, their choice of activity or venue simply costs money that you do not want to or cannot afford to spend.

> *Inaction breeds doubt and fear. Action breeds confidence and courage. If you want to conquer fear, do not sit home and think about it. Go out and get busy.*
>
> **– Dale Carnegie**

The good news is that when it comes to making drastic lifestyle changes—such as deciding to sell your car, cutting restaurants out of the budget altogether, and forgoing lavish vacations until you are out of debt—the only person stopping you is *you*. You do not have to answer to anyone else, nor do you have to deal with your ex-spouse's bad financial decisions or reckless spending. In other words, the person looking back at you in the mirror will not give you pushback about anything you decide to cut out of your life while you are working on getting out of debt. You, and you alone, make those decisions.

The bad news is that the only person generating income for your household is that same person looking back at you in the mirror. When you were married, you and your spouse each had a shovel to dig out of a hole. Now you are down to one shovel, and that brings its own set of challenges. An injury, layoff, or unexpected expense can derail your plan since you can no longer rely on anyone other than yourself to contribute to your household income. If anything, this should scare you. But it should also motivate you.

Fear can be an incredible motivator. If you are reading this, scared to death about your finances, and driven to make changes out of fear, I can relate to that feeling. The best advice I have for you is to harness that emotion and use it to your benefit. It will allow you to make significant lifestyle changes and sacrifices without reservation. Those who are comfortable living with massive amounts of debt are unlikely to make any sort of modifications to their lifestyle.

> *There's a good place to go when you're broke:*
> *To work.*
>
> **– Dave Ramsey**

Depending on your new household income relative to the amount of debt you have, substantial and sweeping changes may be exactly what the doctor has ordered. Again, the good news here is that you no longer have to listen to your former partner complain that you work too much or that it is absurd to cut out cable and restaurants from your life. If you need to pick up overtime or a second job[8] to get out of debt and jump-start your financial recovery, do it. The extreme sacrifice and intensity needed to get out of debt are only temporary.

————————●————————

Spousal support (aka alimony) should not be used to maintain your former lifestyle.

One of the main philosophical arguments that led to state governments passing laws regarding spousal support is that the lower-earning ex-spouse from a lengthy marriage should be able to "maintain the lifestyle" they enjoyed during the union after the divorce is finalized. In reality, if you are the recipient of spousal support, this is the exact opposite of how you should view it. Ideally, spousal support should be used to clean up any debt in your name and bridge any gaps in your budget while you work to gain the education, skills, and experience necessary to boost your income as much as possible by the time the court-ordered support obligation expires.

In most instances, spousal support—if ordered—is only temporary. Even if you are awarded "permanent" spousal support, the truth is that the payment of money into your bank account each month is never guaranteed. Remember that even if your ex-spouse is ordered to pay you a sum of money every

---

8. As recently as a few years ago, taking on a second job was burdensome in ways beyond doing the job itself—especially in light of the time and expense of a commute and childcare costs. These costs call into question the real value of the paycheck from that second job. Yet, the concept of what we think of as a workplace has changed so much in recent years it is easier than ever to find second jobs that can fit your skills and schedule without ever leaving your home.

month, you may not get it. That means that if your mortgage or rent payment is dependent upon your ex-spouse's mandated financial contribution, there is always a risk that the money may not show up when you are expecting it.

I have seen scores of post-decree cases involving nonpayment of spousal support due to the obligor's job loss, temporary disability, permanent disability, or outright refusal to comply with the court order. Just think about 2020 and how a pandemic impacted the economy and unemployment rates. If your ex-spouse loses their job, you will not get paid, which may severely jeopardize your ability to keep a roof over your head if you rely upon those funds to make your house payment. Therefore, it is a good idea to treat the period you receive spousal support as a race against the clock—not the time to live a temporarily inflated lifestyle until that clock stops.

During the time you receive spousal support, one of the best things you can do with the money is to invest in yourself to increase your earning potential. You may have to go back to school to get a better degree, obtain a certification, or acquire specialized training. So long as the training and education yield you a higher paying job, the program's cost will be worth it in the long run. Not all advanced degrees are worth the cost. If you are going to spend your time and money acquiring a degree, certification, or specialized training, you need to make sure that your credentials are in-demand in the marketplace, and the higher salary is virtually guaranteed. You must also commit to getting through the program by paying cash and taking on no student loan debt. Remember, the point is to get out of debt, not to accumulate more.

To illustrate, consider the case of Roy and Pam, and Pam's income post-divorce:

Roy is ordered to pay Pam spousal support at a rate of $1,500 per month for four years. After four years, Pam will see a significant reduction in her monthly income since her only source of funds will be her job. If Pam makes $36,000 per year, assuming no raises, her income will be as follows:

Income Support Total
Year 1: $36,000 + $18,000 = $54,000
Year 2: $36,000 + $18,000 = $54,000
Year 3: $36,000 + $18,000 = $54,000
Year 4: $36,000 + $18,000 = $54,000
Year 5: $36,000 + $0 = $36,000

The absolute *worst* thing Pam could do during the four years she is due to receive spousal support is to live like she is making $54,000 per year. Instead, Pam is on the clock; she has 48 months to get out of debt, boost her skills and education, and do everything in her power to increase her income. Otherwise, when spousal support expires, Pam is going to be in for a rude awakening. She will see her annual household income drop by 1/3 if she does nothing in the meantime to raise her wages. As such, every dollar of spousal support that Pam does not invest in her education, debt reduction, or in some manner to improve her future is a wasted opportunity.

Pam's best course of action is to become acclimated to living off her income of $36,000. If she has any post-divorce debt, she needs to eliminate that by squeezing every dollar she can out of her budget, including using the spousal support to pay off debt. Her $36,000 salary will go much further if she is free from having to make payments for credit cards, a car, and other monthly payments that will otherwise bleed her wallet dry. Being debt-free will ensure that whatever she brings home as income is not siphoned off by creditors every month after her cushion of spousal support terminates. After Pam extinguishes her debt, her primary focus should be on bolstering her career.

With the extra $18,000 a year for four years that Pam receives in spousal support (a total of $72,000), she can afford to pay to obtain a degree or certification, even while maintaining her full-time job. Some will read this and say: *"That's outrageous. She's dealing with a divorce! How can she possibly work full-time AND complete an online program to get her degree when her focus should be on her emotional recovery?!"* My response is that there is always an excuse *not* to do something. Pam certainly has the right to spend the spousal support as she pleases, but she will have nobody to blame but herself if she sees her household income stay stagnant after spousal support stops.

Furthermore, it is entirely possible for someone recovering from divorce to work a full-time job *and* go to school for a degree or certification through many online and evening programs. Many part-time, evening, and online programs exist to accommodate people like Pam. Nobody ever said that this was going to be easy.

> *No discipline seems pleasant at the time, but painful.*
> *Later on, however, it produces a harvest of righteousness.*
> **Hebrews 12:11**

If Pam uses the money she receives as spousal support to eliminate her debts, increase her education, and supercharge her earning ability, she will not face financial ruin at the end of the court-ordered timeframe, or if her former partner, Roy, misses a support payment. Pam will also come out on the other side of her divorce fully capable of counting on herself and earning a higher income than she ever would have in her career at the time she got divorced. Plus, with no debt, Pam will be able to bolster her retirement savings, put away money for college for her children, make additional principal payments on her house for an early payoff, and be in a position to be generous to others.

In many states, spousal support can be reduced or even terminated upon the recipient's cohabitation in a marriage-type relationship; it is terminable upon the recipient's remarriage in almost every state. Sadly enough, I have seen several instances where people have delayed their engagement or marriage to a new partner because they couldn't afford to lose the spousal support they received from their ex-spouse. I can only hope you follow this advice, so you never find yourself in such a grim position. It is heartbreaking to see someone unable to move forward with a new relationship because they are financially beholden to the support paid by their ex-spouse.

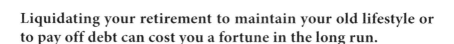

Liquidating your retirement to maintain your old lifestyle or to pay off debt can cost you a fortune in the long run.

One of the worst financial mistakes I regularly see divorcees make is liquidating their retirement before age 59.5 to maintain their prior lifestyle or pay off debt. When I witness people doing this, I cringe because I think of the devastating impact this short-sided decision will have on their future. If you decide to follow in their footsteps and pull money from retirement prematurely, this decision will hurt you in two ways: (1) you will pay penalties and taxes (a 10% penalty *plus* your current income tax rate), which will significantly reduce the net amount you receive, and (2) you miss out on the growth of the money withdrawn, which after years and years of compounding interest will greatly exceed the amount you withdraw now.

An early withdrawal—meaning before age 59.5—from your 401k, 457, 403b, or IRA will require you to pay taxes on your withdrawn amount as if it is income. Plus, you will be responsible for a 10% early withdrawal penalty. For example, if your tax rate is 25%, you will have 35% (your 25% tax rate + a 10% early withdrawal penalty) of the money you are withdrawing from retirement ripped from you right off the top. Thus, a $10,000 early withdrawal would net you $6,500 after penalties and taxes in this scenario. It is essentially the same as borrowing at 35% interest, which is something you would never do unless you needed to avoid foreclosure or bankruptcy.

Your money in a retirement account, so long as it is properly invested—say in a low-cost index fund that tracks the S&P 500—will continue to grow until the day you decide to withdraw it once you are of retirement age. If you have $10,000 invested in an S&P 500 index fund at age 40 and that fund earns 8% compounded interest over 30 years, at age 70, it will be worth $109,000. Consequently, taking this money out of retirement prematurely to pay off $6,500 worth of debt or subsidize an out-of-control budget is an unwise move. While Part II of this book advocates a plan to get rid of debt as fast as possible, it is not suggested that you drain any retirement funds to pay down debt because doing so would irreparably rob from your future retirement.

"Love Your Life, Not Theirs."

We live in an internet-driven culture where everyone else's life seems perfect because of their carefully curated and handpicked online posts. Before your divorce, you may have posted lots of pictures on social media that showed you as a carefree world traveler or a foodie who frequently ate fancy meals at expensive restaurants. You may have posted photographs of concerts and sporting events you attended, as well as pictures of luxury items and even artistic leaves crafted into the foam of your latté. These pictures were all taken when your household income was much higher than it is now, post-divorce. That level of luxury is over until you wipe out your debt and increase your income to that same or a greater level than you had while married. You simply cannot continue to maintain the same life you lived pre-divorce on significantly less income. This includes your "online life."

> *May your life be as awesome as you pretend it is on Facebook.*
>
> **– Unknown**

I recommend reading the book *Love Your Life, Not Theirs: 7 Money Habits for Living the Life You Want* by Rachel Cruze. In her book, Cruze addresses methods to help you avoid the toxic mindset of keeping up with everyone you see on Facebook and Instagram. You may find yourself spending more time on social media, which, in turn, might lead you to believe even more so that everyone else is living a perfect life. I will save you the suspense—they, most unequivocally, are not. Nevertheless, the act of regularly subjecting yourself to these polished images can play tricks on your mind.

One of the most potent aspects of *Love Your Life, Not Theirs* is the running theme of the contentment principle. Advertising focuses on what is missing from your life; its sole purpose is to convince you that you will be more fulfilled if you just buy the product being peddled. While advertising is transparent about what it is trying to accomplish, social media, on the other hand, is not. It has instead generated the unintended consequence of causing you, the unsuspecting consumer, to see all the fun and exciting things everyone else is doing, the picturesque places they are visiting, the products they are buying, the cars they are driving, and the high-end restaurants they are patronizing—all while you are sitting at home, doing nothing more than staring at your phone.

> *I'm so much cooler online.*
>
> **– "Online," a song by Brad Paisley**

If you get caught up trying to live your post-divorce life like everyone else appears to live their lives on social media—by taking vacations you cannot afford, frequently dining out at restaurants when it is not in your budget, attending every concert that rolls through town, and otherwise engaging in retail therapy—you will assuredly stifle your financial recovery. Living this kind of lifestyle means that you are not living on a budget or following a plan. Even worse, if you are not living beneath your means, you are likely relying on debt, your retirement funds, or court-ordered spousal support to bridge the gap between your income and lifestyle.

Although initially challenging, the mistake of trying to maintain the same lifestyle you lived during your marriage is certainly avoidable. If you are going to jump-start your post-divorce financial recovery journey, your lifestyle must conform to your new budget. This requires hard work, sacrifice, and change. The fruits of your labor will be well worth it in the long run, and your future self will thank you for the changes you made—starting today.

Mistake #2:

Insist on Keeping the Marital Residence After Your Divorce

While the costs of the food and beverages you consume, the clothes you wear, and the car you drive can collectively slow your progress, it is the place you call home that has the greatest potential of bringing your financial recovery to a grinding halt.[9]

Without question, the most disastrous financial mistake that I frequently witness in my legal practice is someone insisting on keeping the marital residence post-divorce. Most of the time, the math does not work because their new household income is too low relative to the cost of the real estate. The better financial move tends to be either: (1) receiving 50% of the value of the equity based upon an appraisal and letting their soon-to-be ex-spouse retain the home, or (2) putting it up for sale and dividing the net proceeds. Yet, because of how emotionally connected most people are with their house, this is never an easy conversation. In fact, it is this discussion where I tend to get the most pushback from my clients.

---

9. If you rent and/or if your divorce is over, this section is still 100% applicable to you. Your housing expense is the biggest line item in your budget. If too much of your monthly income is going right out the door to your mortgage lender or landlord, you are going to be handcuffed in your ability to pay down debt and save. As such, while this section is specifically tailored for those who are in the middle of a divorce and contemplating keeping the house and those who have kept the house post-divorce, the bigger issue—which is applicable to *everyone*—is the expense of your housing. The general message is that you may have to move if your housing payment is too much for your income.

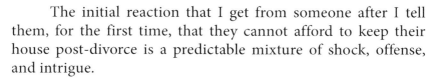

The initial reaction that I get from someone after I tell them, for the first time, that they cannot afford to keep their house post-divorce is a predictable mixture of shock, offense, and intrigue.

There is an unfortunate and recognizable shock that appears on someone's face after hearing that they cannot afford to keep their house. As an adult, can you remember the last time you were told you couldn't afford something? In America, "monthly payments" are synonymous with "affordability"— which irrationally equates to *"if you can afford the monthly payments without going bankrupt, you can 'afford' to buy it."* It is no secret that lenders and banks tailor their teaser interest rates and stretch out the payment timetable to make the monthly payments low enough that otherwise unaffordable products magically become "affordable." If you go to your nearest car dealership and tell them that you want to buy a car today, the odds of you being told *"you can't afford this!"* are slim to none. Instead, the salesperson will do everything in their power to find a lender willing to give you a car loan at an elongated term so the monthly payment becomes low enough that you can "afford" it. This is not isolated to car dealerships either. Financing is available on just about every product imaginable, whether directly from the seller, a third-party lender affiliated with the seller, or a credit card provider.

Next, after the initial shock starts to wear off, the reaction morphs into offense, and their body language seems to translate into *"how dare you!"* Again, this type of exchange in our society is so uncommon that my candor on this subject often catches people off-guard.

Finally, I see intrigue on their faces, as if I am the first person to tell them that keeping the house is a bad financial move in light of their post-divorce household income—because, in most cases, I am. It never ceases to amaze me that before I point out the obvious unaffordability, no one from their support network—not their parents, confidants, close friends, siblings, coworkers, or even their financial advisor—has told them that it would be financially ruinous based on their post-divorce income.

After delivering the news they do not want to hear, I lay out all of the reasons that it is in their best interest to let go of the house and take their share of the equity instead. Emotion trumps none of the reasons.

Reason #1: A math problem is still a math problem, regardless of your emotions.

The most obvious reason not to keep the house following a divorce is that it is too expensive based on your sole income. If you are like most people, when you first went house hunting with your ex-spouse, you started by figuring out what you could afford based on your combined incomes. Your incomes together determined your buying power, which led you to the price point of houses to look at and eventually purchase. Unfortunately, there is no escaping the reality that your post-divorce household income is now less. Typically, much less.

For years, Dave Ramsey has acknowledged only one exception to his "never borrow money" mantra. Taking out a loan is acceptable when it comes to buying a house so long as: (1) you are otherwise debt-free, and (2) the house payment is no more than 25% of your take-home pay on a 15-year fixed-rate mortgage. Dave's home affordability guidelines apply regardless of your life circumstances or emotions and eclipse all excuses you may use to justify buying (or keeping post-divorce) a house that costs you 30%, 40%, or even 50% of your take-home pay.[10]

I certainly understand the emotional attachment to one's home. I also understand the emotional pain caused by divorce. However, just because you have experienced an unexpected life change and might be having a difficult time emotionally, **you do not get a pass on math** when it comes to your home.

I have heard every justification imaginable from clients who want to keep the marital residence post-divorce despite their obvious math problem. Some of the most common explanations are:

- *But this is my dream home!*
- *I can't find anything else to purchase in my price range because there are no other available homes.*
- *There is nowhere else to live in this school district!*
- *I don't want to deal with the expense and hassle of moving!*
- *My monthly mortgage payment on this house will be cheaper than renting!*
- *I don't want to disrupt my children's lives by moving them out of our home!*

In your new post-divorce world, none of these excuses are acceptable. The only way you can afford to keep the house is if your post-divorce income is high enough for you to comply with the guideline that your mortgage payment cost *no more than*

---

10. For renters, the same logic applies. If you spend 30%, 40%, or even 50% of your take-home pay on rent, you are in the same precarious position as someone whose mortgage payment devours a substantial portion of their income. Your ability to pay down debt is contingent upon how much money you have in your budget after all your needs are covered. Naturally, the more money you pay for the roof over your head, the less money you have to pay down your credit cards, car loan, student loans, and consumer debt. It is also less money you have to save for your children's college funds and your own retirement.

25% of your take-home pay on a 15-year fixed-rate mortgage. If you cannot meet this guideline, the house is too expensive for you to keep. Period.

Counting on child and/or spousal support to make your mortgage payment puts your home at risk.

As discussed in Mistake #1, your ex-spouse's payment of support is not guaranteed. Your state has presumably passed laws that mandate criminal repercussions for parents who are substantially behind on their child support. Unfortunately, so many parents are behind on their support obligations that legislatures across the country have determined the penalty of jail time is necessary to get them to pay.

If you are new to the world of child support or spousal support, you may not have encountered the "Deadbeat Ex." I have encountered too many Deadbeat Ex cases to count in my years of practice. On average, my office gets at least one telephone call per day from someone inquiring about initiating an action against a Deadbeat Ex who owes them money, or by a Deadbeat Ex who seeks representation in an enforcement proceeding. In other words, a court order requiring your ex-spouse to pay you money is not a guarantee that you will get paid by the date you need to make your mortgage payment.

The bank that holds the promissory note on your home does not care about *why* you are late on your mortgage payment; if you rent, neither does your landlord. To them, it does not matter if the delinquency of your payment falls squarely on the shoulders of your Deadbeat Ex, nor does it matter that they violated a court order requiring payment of support to you. A late payment is a late payment. Your Deadbeat Ex's nonpayment is *your* problem, not your lender's problem.

You have a contractual obligation to make your mortgage payment every month. Under the typical home loan, if you fail to make your mortgage payment for three months, the bank can file a foreclose action on your home. If you think the divorce court will be able to intervene to stop the foreclosure, you are mistaken.

Moreover, your receipt—or quite possibly, non-receipt—of child support or spousal support can fluctuate based on a variety of factors outside of your control. For instance, if your ex-spouse becomes unemployed, incapacitated, disabled, or flees the country, the money you are counting on to make your house payment will not be there when it is due.

Additionally, spousal support is commonly ordered for a set number of months. For most spousal support recipients, it is only a temporary income stream that will not last the duration of a 15-year mortgage term. So, if you are wholly reliant upon receiving that spousal support to make your mortgage payment, how are you going to pay for the last ten years of your 15-year mortgage if your spousal support runs out in five?

Your divorce decree[11] identifies the extent of the court's jurisdiction to modify the amount of support. If your spouse gets hurt on the job, laid off from work, or retires, depending on the decree's wording, your spousal support award may be suspended or even terminated by the court. Similarly, child support is always modifiable and can hinge upon your children's custodial arrangement and ages. The court retains jurisdiction over your children—and therefore the ability to order child support—until

---

11. Since divorce is handled by the states and not the federal government, state law governs divorces. There are state-specific divorce laws in each of the 50 states, plus the U.S. Territories. Nevertheless, in every state and territory, the court issues an order that spells out each party's rights, obligations, duties, and entitlements with regards to assets, debts, support, and custody if there are children. Each state has a different name for this court order, so, in your case, the controlling document may be called a separation agreement, judgement entry, final decree of divorce, or bear some other name. For the sake of uniformity, I refer to the controlling document as the "divorce decree."

they reach the age of majority (when a child becomes an adult in the eyes of the law or is emancipated). If during that time the custodial arrangement changes, the amount of the child support can change, and so can the party ordered to pay.

Your mortgage is a fixed amount that is due on a set date. Under the terms of your promissory note, you are contractually obligated to make a non-modifiable, predetermined payment each month. If you rely on child support to make your mortgage payment, what happens if your child support is lowered, eliminated, or *you* become the parent obligated to pay? Nothing good, I can assure you.

If the only way you can afford the house is through receipt of child support or spousal support from your ex-spouse, your home is susceptible to risk because of the many variables outside your control. You should certainly include any child and spousal support you receive in your monthly budget but not in your analysis of whether your post-divorce house payment is less than 25% of your take-home pay on a 15-year fixed-rate mortgage. Ask yourself:

> *Do I want to risk the roof over my head and my children's heads based entirely on my ex-spouse's ability to keep a job, stay healthy, stay clean, be responsible, and follow the court's orders?*

Considering that you are no longer married to that person and does not involve the roof over their head, I would not recommend it.

Homeownership is much more costly than the monthly mortgage payment.

Anyone who has ever owned a home knows about the "joys" of being a homeowner when something breaks. When you are a homeowner, the landlord is the person staring back at you in the mirror. So, when your water heater goes out, you get to pay for it. When your roof leaks, it is not only your logistical problem but also your financial responsibility. I remind my clients and people who I financially coach that any roof, foundation, HVAC, and plumbing repair bills can come with multiple 000's tacked on the end. When you are a renter, those repairs are not your problem—they are your landlord's financial and logistical responsibility. But when you are the homeowner, repairs and even regular maintenance expenses can be financially exhausting. Any homeowner whose income is too low relative to the house's cost will struggle to pay for a new HVAC system when the old one needs to be replaced.

If you do not have money set aside in an emergency fund and your furnace stops working in the dead of winter, you will find yourself signing next to the X on the credit application to finance the repair or replacement. Then, for the next 36 to 60 months, you will have to make monthly payments to a creditor. This does nothing more than chip away at your monthly budget and is precisely what we are trying to avoid. Nevertheless, this situation is unavoidable when your house payment eats up too much of your take-home pay.

Emotion is not going to solve your math problem, and it is certainly not going to fix a broken furnace in the middle of winter. Being "house poor" means you will be susceptible to taking on debt because you will not have the wiggle room in your budget to cover the home repairs that you will eventually need to make.

So, how do we strip the emotion out of our analysis? After all, we are talking about the place you call home. To help you see the light, let's look at things from a different perspective.

Ask it in reverse.

During his radio show, Dave Ramsey frequently helps callers who inquire whether they should keep or sell something—such as a home, rental property, boat, car, toy, or investment—walk through the mental gymnastics of their dilemma by asking them to "consider the situation in reverse," as if they did not already own the item in question:

> *Dave [to the caller]: If you didn't own the* _____
> *[home, rental property, car, toy, or item you are unsure*
> *whether you should keep or sell], would you go out*
> *and buy that particular thing today?*

This simple method answered the question from the caller living in California who asked Dave whether he should sell his former residence in Texas, which he had made into a rental by default when he was transferred by his employer 1,000 miles westward. When presented with this fact pattern, Dave asked: "If you did not own this house in Texas, and you wanted to buy a rental property while you were living in California, would you buy a rental property a thousand miles away in Texas?" Of course not.

There is a genius to this straightforward and simple idea of asking something in reverse: it points out the apparent answer without condescension or emotion. Inevitably, the caller concluded—with a slight nudge from Dave—that it would be absurd for him to buy rental real estate 1,000 miles away because he would have no way to keep an eye on the property, screen tenants, or attend to it in any reasonable manner without using hired help. The rare exception occurs when a caller tells Dave that the item in question is irreplaceable because it is a childhood home or a piece of property that has been in the bloodline for generations.

Even though the marital residence is rarely a generational property, in my experience, I have found that it nonetheless elicits a strong emotional connection for many people going through a divorce. This may include you. Understandably, the place that you call home represents stability during a tumultuous period in your life. But that feeling of comfort does not solve your math problem. In my practice, I tend to use Dave's tactic of asking the question in reverse for clients who initially say they want to keep the house, albeit against my advice, by emphasizing their projected post-divorce household income:

> *If you did not own this particular house and you were in the market to buy a home with your post-divorce, single-source income, would you be interested in purchasing this specific house at this price point?*

Almost universally, the answer is *no*. Occasionally, clients will tell me that they would certainly buy this particular house, and they even have a lender lined up to give them a loan they can "afford." Unfortunately, the loan they describe tends to be on a 30-year term (or even worse, it's an adjustable-rate loan with a teaser interest rate)—and for their plan to work, nothing in the house can ever break because they cannot afford any repairs due to so much of their income being gobbled up by the house payment.

> *The rich rule over the poor, and the borrower is slave to the lender.*
>
> **Proverbs 22:7**

One of the reasons the 30-year mortgage is so popular in the U.S. is because it lowers the monthly house payment compared to the 15-year alternative. Long ago, bankers figured out that stretching the term of any loan is doubly effective. It procures a greater amount of interest for the lender and creates a larger pool of borrowers who can presumably "afford" the lower monthly payments.

A homebuyer who takes out a $200,000 mortgage on a 30-year loan with a fixed rate of 5% will pay a total of $386,500 to own the home: $200,000 in principal + $186,500 in interest over the 30-year life of the loan.

Conversely, a homebuyer who takes out a $200,000 mortgage on a 15-year loan with a fixed rate of 4.5%[12] will pay $275,400 to own that home: $200,000 in principal + $75,400 in interest over the 15-year life of the loan. That is a difference of over $110,000:

$386,500 (total of the principal & interest paid on a 30-year loan)
-$275,400 (total of the principal & interest paid on a 15-year loan)

$111,100 SAVED by using a 15-year vs. a 30-year loan.

Not only does the 15-year mortgage save the homebuyer $111,100 in interest compared to the 30-year mortgage, but the house is paid off *15 years earlier.*

Your monthly mortgage payment could be higher post-divorce.

The marital residence tends to be the largest asset to be divided in a divorce. Consequently, the person keeping the house must often pursue a cash-out refinance to have the funds available to pay one-half of the marital equity to the other person. As part of the refinancing, a new underwriting process takes place and a new loan is issued, which may have a higher interest rate and monthly payment. Furthermore, whereas your prior loan was underwritten using your spouse's income and credit score, this time around, your sole income and credit score

---

12. The interest rates on 15-year fixed-rate mortgages are typically 0.5% less than the interest rates on 30-year fixed-rate mortgages.

will be used by the bank to determine your creditworthiness and, in turn, interest rate.

To illustrate the post-divorce math involved with keeping the house, consider Pam's situation:

> *Roy and Pam are going through a divorce. They owe $100,000 on their $200,000 house, meaning the house has $100,000 of marital equity. Therefore, each party is entitled to $50,000 of equity. If Pam wants to keep the house, she will have to pay Roy $50,000. Since there are no other sizable liquid assets to pay Roy this sum, Pam will have to refinance the property solely into her name and do a cash-out refinance with the $50,000 she owes Roy rolled into her new loan. As such, her new loan balance will be $150,000 (which is comprised of the current $100,000 mortgage balance + $50,000 she will receive from the bank to pay Roy his share of the equity). Unfortunately, Pam cannot assume she'll get the same 15-year loan that she and Roy locked in at 2.75% when they purchased it in 2015, and she will be subject to the current rate at the time of her refinancing.*

With Roy no longer in the picture, Pam is the sole source of income for her household. She must figure out whether a $150,000 mortgage on her salary is not just doable but reasonable—meaning it must be less than or equal to 25% of her take-home pay on a 15-year fixed-rate mortgage.

> *At a 4.25% interest rate on a 15-year fixed-rate mortgage, the best rate Pam can get with a cash-out refinance at the time, her mortgage payment on a $150,000 mortgage (not including property taxes and homeowners insurance) is $1,128 per month. Add in*

property taxes and insurance, and Pam's post-divorce house payment will be approximately $1,500 per month.

Therefore, applying the principles previously outlined, for Pam to reasonably afford this house—under the 25% of her take-home pay on a 15-year fixed-rate mortgage guideline—her net pay (after income taxes, insurance, and withholdings) needs to be greater than or equal to $6,000 per month. If Pam's monthly take-home pay is anything less, she will struggle to get ahead financially because too much of her monthly budget will be going to housing.

Pam does not get a pass on math, and neither do you. You no longer have the luxury of counting on your ex-spouse's income, and if you purchased your home based on having that income in your budget, you need to rerun the numbers with only your sole income to see if you fall within the prescribed guideline.

Therefore, if keeping the marital home will tie up too much of your monthly income, and it falls outside of the *25% of your take-home pay on a 15-year fixed-rate mortgage* guideline, you cannot afford to keep it.

----◆----

Reason #2: The house has baggage.

It does not take a doctorate degree in psychology to recognize that your marital residence has baggage. Even worse, if you keep the home, you welcome that old baggage into your new post-divorce life. Your kitchen, master bedroom, family room, and other areas of your home have likely been places where you have had arguments, shed tears, stewed in anger, and felt extreme levels of frustration. So long as you live in that house, you will have regular in-your-face reminders of bad times, broken promises, quarrels, and contention. As stated previously, I am not a mental health expert. But what I do know is that subjecting yourself daily to the scenes of the worst times in your marriage makes it difficult to start fresh.

If I apply the tool of "asking it in reverse," not from a financial and affordability perspective but an emotional standpoint, it underscores this point:

> *If you did not own this house, would you be in the market for a home that serves as a daily reminder to you of some of the worst moments in your life?*

This question is meant to be a bit absurd because, frankly, I am not sure anyone would answer affirmatively. Every other house in your area has the benefit of being unencumbered by the baggage that is forever tied to your marital home. I encourage you to keep this in mind if you are still of the belief that you want to keep it.

Reason #3: You need to find the right fit based on your needs post-divorce.

In my experience, the occasional times when a client can continue to afford to keep the marital residence occurs when the divorce is later in life, after many years of marriage, and the parties have accumulated substantial wealth (net worth of over $1 million) while living in a modestly-priced residence. In those few instances where affordability is not an issue, the fit seems to be the more significant area of concern. Therefore, even if you can afford to keep the marital residence, and even if you believe that continuing to live there post-divorce will have no impact on your mental health, you must still ask yourself: *"Is this home the right fit for me at this point in my life?"*

I will never forget a former client of mine, Kate, who was all set to walk away from her divorce with a substantial monthly spousal support award, in addition to property and financial accounts worth nearly $2.5 million. At the time of her divorce, Kate was 59 years old. She had been married to her husband for 36 years, and all four of their children were grown and out of the house. At the outset of her case, Kate initially told me she wanted to keep her five-bedroom, 4,000 square-foot home that sat on an acre of land. Kate could certainly afford to keep the house, as there were enough assets in the marriage that her ex-husband could take other property and accounts to offset the marital residence's value without her having to take out a mortgage on the property. While Kate could continue to live in the home and afford the expense of maintaining it, she was nonetheless an empty-nester.

When I asked her why she wanted to keep such a big house, Kate explained that she liked celebrating Christmas Eve in the den where she and her family had always opened presents before and eating Christmas dinner around the same dining room table for all those years. Indeed, the holiday memories were so positive and vibrant in Kate's mind that she convinced herself the home was worth keeping.

I then asked Kate about maintaining the lawn, flowerbeds, heating, cooling, cleaning, and general upkeep of the house. At this question, the emotional part of Kate's mind—which had been focused on the good times that occurred two days out of the year—was overtaken by the rational part. Recounting the woes of keeping up with this big, empty, lonely house reminded her that the remaining 363 days would be filled with many hours of labor that would outweigh any joy she felt while hosting family holiday celebrations on December 24th and 25th.

The reality is that if Kate did not own this particular house and was instead in the market for something to buy as a newly single empty nester, she would *not* be in the market for a five-bedroom, 4,000 square foot house on an acre of land. Although she could handle the financial responsibilities of it, she could also avoid the time and effort needed to maintain the property by choosing to let it go. Ultimately, she made the smart decision, and the house was put up for sale. When it sold, she was able to buy a smaller house, for cash, that fit her post-divorce lifestyle.

Using Kate's situation for perspective, even if you can afford to keep the marital residence, ask yourself the question (again in reverse, but considering your lifestyle needs):

If I did not own my current house—when considering the cost, square footage, and amount of upkeep—is this the house I would be looking to buy given what my life is going to look like after divorce?

Only you can determine the perfect size, location, and price point for your new living situation. It may be too soon for you to understand what your needs will be post-divorce. Renting might be a good, temporary solution—especially if you need to pay off debt. It will mean you have a predictable, fixed monthly housing expense since the landlord is responsible for any repairs. It will also give you a short-term solution to your housing needs without stretching your budget too thin or locking you into a situation that may be difficult or costly to escape. Renting buys you time while you search for the perfect place based upon your lifestyle, budget, location, and needs.

Your ultimate goal should be to live in a paid-for house that you own—not one that owns you.

***

Reason #4: Bad timing can make a world of difference.

Like hundreds of thousands of Americans, I was laid off during the Great Recession in 2009. The legal market was so lacking in my hometown that the job I found two months later was in a different state and roughly 100 miles from the house I owned.

I put my house up for sale with the belief that it would only be on the market for a month or two. With this abbreviated and naive timeframe in mind, I kept my furniture there to keep it staged and presentable to prospective buyers. I planned to move all of my furniture, including my bedroom furniture, to my new residence once my house sold. In the meantime, I moved only a few items to the new city and slept on an air mattress because I figured it would be a short term, temporary measure. I realized the flaw in my logic soon enough. Without any grasp of the depths of the recession or any idea how long the depressed housing market would last, I held out hope to get an offer on my house. That offer never came.

Seven months later, I broke down and began renting the house because I could no longer afford to keep it vacant, and it was apparent no offer on the house was forthcoming. I finally moved my furniture and ditched the air mattress but found myself being a landlord by default for several years thereafter because it took that long for the housing market to recover fully.

When I discuss with my clients the issue of keeping the marital residence, I am often met with the response of: *"If it doesn't work out or I can't afford it, I'll just put it up for sale."* However, if keeping the house means you will be financially stretched every month, the concept of easily getting rid of it *"if it becomes too much"* may not be so easy. Like countless others in 2009 and 2010, I could not seem to sell my house at a time I desperately wanted to get rid of it. An event entirely outside of your control—like a major employer leaving your city, a layoff from work that halts your income, or an economic recession— can derail your backup plan to offload the house quickly and at a great price. Your alternative of having to put the house up for sale at a distressed price, just so you can offload it, could be financially devastating.

Beyond timing, there are two other issues that you must consider if you plan to keep the house post-divorce: (1) the valuation used during the divorce, and (2) the commission you will have to pay to sell it.

First, if you wish to keep the house post-divorce, you need to hire a licensed appraiser to ensure you do not overpay. In my practice, I have seen attorneys associate with only one particular appraiser who either comes in "high" or "low" depending on the interest of their client. Therefore, accepting a valuation based solely on an appraisal that was obtained by your spouse's attorney during the divorce, without obtaining an independent assessment of your own, could mean you end up overpaying for the house. Still, an appraisal is just an educated opinion of what the home will sell for based upon past sales of comparable homes in the area. Accordingly, appraisers have difficulty adjusting for sudden and dramatic market changes due to a recession, nearby plant or office closure, or interest rate hike—all of which can have an impact that makes previously-sold houses under different market conditions much less reliable as a basis for comparison.

Second, if you initially keep the house but at any point thereafter decide to sell it after the divorce is finalized, you are going to be solely responsible for bearing the entire realtors' commission. This is typically six percent of the sales price (three percent to the buyer's agent and three percent to the listing agent). Conversely, if you sell the house during the divorce, your ex-spouse will be responsible for half the commission expense. The difference is three percent of the sales price, which can be substantial. On a $250,000 house sale, you are splitting the $15,000 realtors' commissions with your soon-to-be-ex-spouse (at $7,500 each) when you sell it together, or you are eating the entire $15,000 cost yourself if you keep the house during the divorce but end up selling it later. Depending on the house's sale price and the amount of debt that you are going to be responsible for once the divorce is finalized, this can be a hefty sum of money that must be considered in your analysis.

To illustrate, consider Michael and Jan's situation:

Michael insisted on keeping the marital home in his divorce. Michael's soon-to-be ex-wife, Jan, who did not want the house, had it appraised by a licensed appraiser of her attorney's choosing. Jan's appraiser reported a valuation of $250,000. Michael opted to save the $350 cost of getting his own appraisal and accepted *the $250,000 valuation. This was a bad decision on Michael's part. Had Michael obtained his own appraisal, he would have found that the assessment obtained by Jan's attorney was $20,000 too high because it relied on old sales in different neighborhoods. The more accurate estimate of $230,000 would have given Michael significant bargaining power and would have resulted in him compensating Jan her share of the equity based upon the market price.*

With a $150,000 mortgage still owed on the property, and the $250,000 valuation, Michael had to do a cash-out refinance to pay Jan an agreed-upon settlement figure of $45,000 to satisfy her share of the supposed equity in the home (which Michael perceived to be a discount from the $50,000 she claimed to be owed).

The appraisal done by the bank at the time of Michael's refinance reported a valuation of $230,000. Yet, because Jan's settlement agreement was already signed and the divorce was finalized, Michael had to swallow this bitter pill and honor his contractual obligation. As such, his new home loan balance was $195,000 ($150,000 balance + $45,000 cash-out = $195,000).

Michael's alternative—before signing the settlement agreement—was to insist that the house be put up for sale. Selling it would have fetched the fair-market price of $230,000, and would have caused the six percent commission, totaling $13,800 (three percent going to the buyer's agent, and three percent going to the listing agent), to be equally borne by both Michael and Jan. Thus, at closing, the net proceeds of $66,200 would have been split, yielding each party a check for $33,100.

$230,000 sales price
- $150,000 mortgage balance
- $13,800 commission
$66,200 / 2 = **$33,100 each to Michael and Jan**

Instead, since Michael kept the house at the inflated price, Jan benefited to the tune of nearly $12,000 more than what she was otherwise entitled.

Two years after the divorce, Michael could no longer handle the expenses associated with owning the house, so he put it up for sale. Unfortunately, the local housing and job markets had both taken a turn for the worse. One of the town's largest employers had laid off 15% of its workforce, and further cuts were anticipated. When Michael listed the house for sale, he did so when there were many other comparable houses for sale and in a community where too many residents were concerned about the stability of their employment.

Michael eventually sold the house at a distressed price of $210,000 and had to pay the entire realtors' commission of $12,600. Since he took out a 30-year mortgage when he refinanced, Michael's loan balance at the time of the sale was $185,000. Therefore, after paying the $12,600 commission, Michael received a check at closing for $12,400.

$210,000 sales price
- $185,000 mortgage balance
- $12,600 commission
$12,400 to Michael

Michael's situation underscores the point that if you are going to get rid of your house, do it during the divorce, not after.

If you only intend to keep it for a short time, you run the risk of overpaying for it, and your equity in the house could be negated by having to pay the entire commission when you go to sell it. Even worse, if you find yourself stretched too thin and subject to the ups and downs of the market, you could get stuck selling it in a buyer's market at a price much less than you can afford to take. This will only set your post-divorce financial recovery back even further.

Reason #5: You want your home to be a blessing, not a curse.

Your house is the largest purchase you will ever make. If you buy a place that is (1) affordable based upon your income and within the guidelines we've discussed, (2) appropriate for your post-divorce lifestyle, and (3) purchased intentionally and not done by default or out of desperation, it can certainly be a blessing to you. Conversely, an overpriced house that makes you "house poor" will inevitably be a curse with long-lasting ramifications. That means your justifications for keeping the house, if you choose to go that route, must be financially grounded and not be driven by emotions.

Choosing to stay in the house "for the benefit of the children" is something I hear quite frequently from clients as a justification. I understand their desire to minimize further disruption in their children's lives on the heels of the divorce. I can also see how one might conclude that their children's familiarity with the house might somehow make the absence of their other parent more tolerable. But a house does not provide love and attention to you as an adult. By the same token, it certainly provides no love or attention to scared, confused, and anxious children who are trying to comprehend what is going on with their parents. While you may be convinced that the continuity of living quarters will provide some sort of comfort and emotional shelter for your children, you need to be aware that every other aspect of their life is now different. The same way this house has baggage for you, it has baggage for them too.

Take comfort in the fact that, like you, your children are resilient. They can survive if they have to pack up all their belongings and move into a different house or apartment, or (*gasp*) share a bedroom with their sibling. To be blunt, your pre-divorce lifestyle provided you with more of a cushion to spend on luxuries that you will not be able to afford post-divorce. Working more hours—which will result in spending less time with your children—just to be able to afford the payments on a house that is beyond your means is not a wise plan for you or them.

Finally, spite is one of the worst reasons imaginable for keeping the marital residence. I am still surprised—although, maybe I shouldn't be at this point—at how often I hear a client or prospective client tell me that they want to keep the marital home because they do not want their soon-to-be ex-spouse to have it. Please, do not make this mistake. Do not saddle yourself with the financial responsibilities of a house out of spite, anger, revenge, or any other emotion.

No matter how hard you try to convince yourself that *this* particular house is your "dream home," and it is the only possible home for you and your kids post-divorce, you need to remember that there is a house on every corner. Take a cold shower and get rid of the house-fever you have developed for this particular property because others will better fit your needs and your budget when you are financially ready to be a homeowner.

If you are still convinced that you want to keep your house after reading all these reasons, nobody is stopping you. It is unlikely your divorce attorney will voice a single word of opposition. Whether you realize it or not, your attorney is in the customer service business and works for you. Happy clients tell other people to use that attorney's services, which, in turn, generates more business referrals. So, if you insist on keeping the house at an inflated value and with a mortgage payment you cannot afford, who is going to stop you? If you think the court is going to stop you from making a bad financial decision, you are mistaken. Also, you can pretty much guarantee that your soon-to-be ex-spouse is not going to stop you from keeping the property when it is financially beneficial to them.

Here is the most troubling part from my perspective: it is possible that even those closest to you will not tell you that you are making a bad financial decision by keeping a residence that will keep you strapped for cash. The reason for their silence is understandable and straightforward—they want you to be happy. If the topic of your home, car, or some other unaffordable item comes up in your conversations and you talk about how happy you are that you can keep any or all of the above, you are not going to hear an objection from them.

Again, I wrote this book because I want to help support network members be equipped to speak up and be honest with their loved ones when they see them about to make a questionable financial decision. So, if someone in your life tries to talk to you about your finances and financial decisions, know that their act of doing so took tremendous courage and comes from a place of love. Listen to their input; do not blindly follow it, but listen to the concerns they are raising. Then think through it logically at a time when you are not overwhelmed by emotion or the conversation. Conversely, do not mistake a loved one's silence as tacit approval of your decision; they may feel ill-equipped to be able to tell you what you need to hear.

Ultimately, a bad financial decision is still a bad financial decision, regardless of your emotions. That is why this book exists—to help you avoid bad financial decisions and to tell you the harsh realities that your loved ones may be unable or unwilling to say.

———————◉———————

If you ended up with the house post-divorce, you could always sell it.

If your divorce is already over, and you ended up with the marital residence, you are not bound to keep it. If, after reading this book in its entirety, you discover that it is too expensive, too much house or too much of a stressor in your life, go ahead and find an energetic realtor in your area who can help you list the house for sale at the right time and price.

We are all human, so we've all made regrettable financial decisions at some point in our lives. There is no shame in reversing course after you have made a bad financial decision. This is a prudent reminder for divorcees, especially when it comes to the marital residence. I have seen too many divorcees try to keep a house out of pride. One client of mine even told me that she wanted to keep living in the house just to "prove" to her former partner that she could do it. I will tell you the same thing I told her: *you have nothing to prove to anyone, especially to your ex-spouse.*

Keeping the marital home can be the greatest mistake in any divorce and can set your post-divorce financial recovery back a decade or longer given its magnitude. The smartest thing you can do if you are in an overly expensive living situation is to make a change as soon as possible. If you wait a year, then the roof, windows, siding, furnace, and every other big-ticket item in the house is just a year older and may need to be repaired or replaced on your dime. Waiting ensures a prolonged period where you have to live on a constricted budget, which in turn delays your ability to free up money so you can aggressively pay off your other debts, save for your retirement, and resume investing in you and your children's future.

Mistake #3:
Retail Therapy

———●———

Whenever one of my clients starts to seek my advice on emotional issues, I use the same timeless line that divorce lawyers have used for decades: *"I'm half as qualified and twice as expensive as a psychologist."* While I am certainly concerned about my clients' mental health, I do not want them to waste their money on having me listen to their emotional issues—while paying my hourly billable rate—since there are professionals who are better suited and more qualified to help them with this aspect of their lives. Yet some situations are so obvious that no psychology degree is needed for me to intervene. Retail therapy is one of them.

"Retail therapy" is defined by the *Cambridge Dictionary* as "the act of buying special things for yourself in order to feel better when you are unhappy."[13] For divorcees, and frankly anyone in debt, the concept of retail therapy is an oxymoron, as it is the perpetrator of a vicious cycle. It is also one of the biggest, yet most easily avoidable, mistakes that I see divorcees make, time and time again.

> *Recreational shopping is the shortest distance*
> *between two points:*
> *You and Broke.*
>
> **– Victoria Moran**

---

13. *Retail therapy*, CAMBRIDGE DICTIONARY ONLINE, https://dictionary.cambridge.org/us/dictionary/english/retail-therapy (last visited 10/4/2020).

Without a doubt, recovering from a divorce is in a totally different galaxy than recovering from a bad day at work. Retail therapy, a glass of wine, and comfort food are all common outlets people use to help themselves get over short-term problems, like having a bad day or a rough week. Those methods of stress relief, however, are unsustainable and dangerous for dealing with longer-term matters, including coping with the life changes following your divorce. You can rely on an umbrella during a rainstorm, but not during a hurricane.

We all know that there are just some days when comfort food does exactly what it was meant to do. You go to bed with a full belly and relaxed mind that is distracted from all the problems of the day. The next morning, you wake up feeling better since the issue that bothered you the night before is now less concerning. That method of coping works if it is used sparingly.

On the contrary, it can have a destructive effect if used excessively. If you eat too much comfort food, soon none of your clothes are going to fit. Putting on weight, in turn, will likely make you disheartened. Then if you once again turn to comfort food to deal with your emotions, that will only make your weight issue worse. Swap in any other short-term coping vice, like drinking alcohol or recreational shopping, and the result is the same when used over a long period of time. If you turn to alcohol to feel better every day, soon you could find yourself relying too much on it and eventually dependent.

Retail therapy as a means of coping with a long-term issue, just to feel better for a fleeting moment in time, is not only unsustainable but a financial time bomb that will eradicate any potential of financial success until it is controlled. You can certainly envision the vicious cycle of spending money just to feel better:

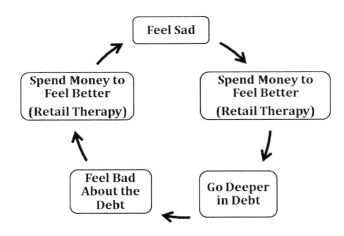

Retail therapy can take many forms, both big and small. For many, it occurs as frequent, superfluous, and therapeutically motivated expenses that add up over time. It can also take much larger forms, including luxury purchases, vehicles, and even your house. As discussed previously, keeping the marital home, for some, is simply an enormous form of retail therapy. Cars can also be a form of retail therapy but with substantially greater financial consequences than a shopping spree at the mall.

A former client of mine, Rebecca, struggled with depression during her divorce. Near the end of her case, Rebecca showed up to a meeting at my office with a smile on her face for the first time in months. She told me she had just picked out the brand-new car she intended to buy after her divorce was finalized. She and her mother had gone car shopping that morning, and Rebecca had test drove a $40,000 car she "just had to have." Rebecca's well-intentioned, kind-hearted mother told me that she was relieved to see her daughter happy about anything for the first time in a year, even though it involved her daughter spending a lot of money (that she didn't have).

Although neither Rebecca nor her mother asked my opinion, I could not help but interject. I explained to them that between Rebecca's $42,000 annual salary and sizable student loan debt, buying a $40,000 car was completely impractical. The difference between my advice and her mother's advice was the absence of emotion. For Rebecca's mother, her emotions were inseparable from her input. Understandably, she was concerned most about her daughter's short-term happiness, as shown by her admission that she was thrilled just to see her daughter smile again. Yet Rebecca's mother expressed little, if any, concern over the long-term consequences of her daughter's overspending on a new car as an obvious form of retail therapy.

Unlike her mother, my guidance was unencumbered by emotion and strictly focused on math. Whereas I had the perspective of an outsider, Rebecca's mother had had to endure seeing her daughter cry and sulk regularly for months on end. If it took a new car to get the tears to stop, Rebecca's mother was not going to be the voice of opposition.

This dynamic between Rebecca and her mother, with regards to financial issues, is something that I have seen too many times to count. Although well-intentioned, I frequently find that family members, friends, and coworkers who provide emotional support to divorcees are ill-equipped, uncomfortable, and even unwilling to have any difficult conversations about their loved one's finances and spending habits. This is certainly understandable, given the dynamic of their relationships.

Picture the faces of those in your support network. They want to see you happy. If buying something makes you happy, many of them will stay silent instead of sharing their thoughts on your spending because your "happiness" is preferable to pain.

They want to see a smile on your face. If Rebecca's mother had confronted her daughter about her retail therapy, she would presumably have felt like an additional source of pain for Rebecca. In their situation, the net result was the willingness of a mother to condone a bad decision by her daughter, which would have hurt her substantially in the long run, just to avoid an immediate but temporary disappointment. **The road to financial hell is paved with the good intentions of those who enable you.**

> *Only enemies speak the truth; friends and lovers lie endlessly, caught in the web of duty.*
>
> **– Stephen King**

If you have friends and family members who are helping you emotionally in your post-divorce recovery, it is quite possible that they have never brought up your spending habits and finances as an in-depth topic of conversation. Even though they may have watched this problem develop in real-time, they might remain silent because they are unwilling, or simply unable, to talk about your finances with you. Sure, some surface-level conversations about money might take place, but is there someone in your life who cares so much about your long-term well-being that they will throw a bucket of cold water on your spending habits? If you have a person like that in your life, consider yourself lucky.

My advice is if you have someone in your life who is capable of being a voice of reason when it comes to your finances and spending habits, ask them to speak up if they see you doing something concerning, irresponsible, or downright stupid. These are the types of accountability partners we need, particularly in times of turmoil. Although their perspective and guidance may be unpleasant to hear, it will be valuable to you in the long run, especially since their voice might be the only one that says what you need to hear. If someone close to you is willing to be forthright, it is worth listening; while their advice may not always be worth following, it is nonetheless helpful to have a second opinion on any financial quandaries you encounter along the way.

If you are still in the process of finalizing your divorce and your attorney prods you on your finances, budget, and/ or spending habits, just remember that their input will soon disappear from your life. The relationship between the divorce attorney and client is of a limited, short-term duration that ends once the divorce decree is granted by the court. Your post-divorce "recovery" will be a work-in-progress even when your attorney's job is complete.

Find an accountability partner.

One of the infrequently discussed challenges of post-divorce life is the lack of an accountability partner—someone who will confront you and hold you accountable when it comes to your budget. When you are single and living alone, no one calls you out on your excessive expenditures. You won't get pushback from anyone in your home if you overspend on shoes, buy a car you cannot afford, or have a daily vice that slowly and steadily drains your wallet. While married, even if you had money fights, there was still a second voice on both major and minor household purchases. That second opinion, capable of checking your behavior, is now gone.

If you are going to be financially successful after your divorce, you need to find someone who can be that second opinion if you struggle to hold yourself accountable. That person can be a coworker, family member, close friend, or someone you know who is good with money and willing to meet with you regularly to help monitor your budget and spending. If no one in your family is proficient with money, and your friends and coworkers aren't any better, consider asking your pastor if they can direct you to an accountability partner. Alternatively, if you enroll in *Financial Peace University* (FinancialPeace.com), you may find someone willing to serve in this role for you as you do the same for them.

The bottom line here is if you find yourself spending money as a means of trying to cope emotionally, you are going to have to break the cycle somehow. Fortunately, mental health professionals are skilled in teaching coping methods that are not self-destructive, so please do not hesitate to seek out professional help before you find yourself engaging in such behavior. It may be the best decision you ever make.

———●———

The best way to track and control your spending is to create a budget and stick to it.

If you are unsure whether you are engaging in retail therapy or not, I can only assume that you do not currently use a budget. If you put one together and follow it, you'll give yourself the freedom to spend according to the plan you set out each month. When you stick to your budget, you allow yourself to spend a predetermined amount of money every month on your wants— say $50, $100, or $200 per month on clothes, shoes, sporting goods, tools, or any item that will make you feel better—without sabotaging your financial recovery. Moreover, because you know exactly where your money is going each month, you'll avoid the emotional distress associated with wondering where it all went. If you are not following a budget, now is the time to start. (Part II of this book will discuss budgeting and freely available resources that can help you stick to your budget.)

Finally, keep in mind that retail therapy is real, and every one of us is susceptible to spending frivolously as a means to deal with our emotions. If you are spending money in order to cope with your divorce, it will end up being much more expensive than the cost of a good counselor. In the long run, retail therapy will keep you in debt, and the root cause of your spending will continue to be unaddressed. It is natural to be upset, angry, frustrated, and hurt by the divorce process and everything you have endured in separating from your ex-spouse. For your own sake, though, and for the sake of your future self, I encourage you to seek proper assistance from those trained in this area and not to use spending as a way to feel some sort of instant, temporary pleasure.

MISTAKE #4:

NOT KNOWING AND ENFORCING THE TERMS
OF YOUR DIVORCE DECREE

A frequent, preventable, and cringe-worthy mistake that divorcees regularly make is not knowing the terms of the controlling document from their divorce (typically the judgment decree or separation agreement) that establishes each party's responsibility for marital debts and delineates parental rights.

I cannot emphasize this enough: You *must* be familiar with the terms of your divorce decree, and you *must* take action if your former partner violates the terms of your decree when it comes to their nonpayment of debts on which you are a co-debtor.

Even if the court issued an order that requires your ex-spouse to pay off a debt that you are contractually obligated to pay, either as the sole debtor or co-debtor, *you are still liable.* Under the terms of the contract, you are still legally responsible for that debt until your ex-spouse: (1) extinguishes your obligation by paying off the debt in full, or (2) refinances the debt solely into their name. If your ex-spouse takes neither of those two actions, you can be sued by the lender, despite the order from the divorce court. In other words, the divorce court's order does not nullify your legal, contractual obligation to the lender on debts where you signed your name to be the primary debtor, co-debtor, or co-signer (also known as a guarantor).

Under the terms of your divorce decree, if your ex-spouse is ordered to pay a debt for which you are contractually liable and they fail to make the payments, it can be an absolute nightmare for you. The only way to prevent it from turning into a horrific situation is by: (1) knowing exactly what is stated in your divorce decree regarding the allocation of responsibilities for debts in your name, and (2) taking immediate action through the court if your ex-spouse fails to do what they are obligated to do in the timeframe required by the court order.

Understandably, most people, including divorcees, have no familiarity whatsoever with their state's laws, the effect of court orders, and the consequences of noncompliance with a court order. I frequently tell my clients that even though the court has issued an order, it does not guarantee performance by their ex-spouse. Court orders are ignored all the time, which is why the court has contempt powers to lock someone up for their failure to comply with a court order. For the court to take action to hold a noncomplying party accountable, the violation of the court order must be brought to the court's attention. In other words, the court does not know what it does not know until you let it know. This is done by filing a motion to hold the other party in contempt (commonly known as a "show cause" motion).

To better explain this issue—and illustrate why this is of critical importance for you—let's look at three examples common to divorcees where one party was noncompliant with an order to refinance or extinguish a debt within a set amount of time: (1) the mortgage on the marital residence; (2) a car loan; and (3) credit card debt.

Example 1—Mortgage on the Marital Residence:

In the divorce between Andy and Angela, the court issued a divorce decree that adopted the parties' agreement that Andy shall retain the marital residence and pay Angela $20,000 to compensate her for her share of the equity. Since Angela's name was on the *home loan, Andy was required to get Angela's name removed by doing one of the following:*

- *Assume the loan, solely in his name, through a written agreement with the lender, which would remove Angela's responsibility on the debt (an infrequent occurrence);*
- *Refinance the mortgage solely into his name; or*
- *Sell the property so the loan in both names would be extinguished.*

The decree gave Andy 90 days to obtain refinancing on the property or assume the loan. If Andy accomplished neither in the 90-day timeframe, he was required to list the property for sale by the 120th day. After the 270th day, Andy was required to sell it at auction. The decree further states that Andy was to make all payments on the house pending refinance, loan assumption, or sale. It also states that in the event of a sale, Andy is entitled to receive any profits from any sale, and he is solely responsible for a deficiency should the sales proceeds be insufficient to cover the balance of the home loan.

One week after the issuance of the divorce decree, Andy paid Angela $20,000.

Yet, one year later, Angela's name was still on the home loan. Andy failed to refinance the property or list it for sale as he was ordered to do under the terms of the decree. Additionally, due to an injury at work, Andy stopped paying on the house and missed three payments. Angela was unaware that Andy failed to refinance the property and assumed that Andy had complied with the divorce decree. Instead, Angela learned of Andy's noncompliance when she was served by the sheriff with a foreclosure lawsuit filed by the lender in which she was named as a defendant because her name was still on the mortgage and promissory note as a co-debtor.

In this example, Angela made two common and avoidable mistakes. First, she failed to keep a close watch on Andy's progress regarding refinancing within the 90-day window he was given by the decree. She could have accomplished this any number of ways, including:

- Periodically contacting Andy directly to ask him the status of the refinancing or sales listing;

- Contacting the lender to see if her name was still on the debt;

- Asking her attorney to contact Andy's attorney to inquire of the status; or

- Pulling her credit report to see if the debt was still listed as outstanding in her name.

Each one of these methods would have required a nominal amount of effort on Angela's part. Furthermore, setting a simple calendar reminder on her phone for the 91st day also could have alerted Angela to Andy's noncompliance, which might have averted this crisis.[14]

Second, Angela erred by not taking immediate action upon Andy's failure to list the house for sale within the timeframe imposed by the divorce decree. By the 91st day, Angela should have contacted Andy to see if he had successfully refinanced

---

14. Without getting into the intricacies of real estate law, which is similar to divorce law in that it is state specific, it is likely that Angela would need to sign a quit claim deed at some point following the divorce, either in association with the refinancing or the sale of the property. By never signing anything releasing her interest in the property, such as a quit claim deed, Angela, again, should have been on notice of her continued attachment to the property.

the mortgage. Upon confirming that he hadn't, Angela should have reminded Andy of his legal obligation to list the house for sale immediately. By the 121st day, if the house had not been listed, Angela could have acted right away to bring Andy's noncompliance to the court's attention, either on her own or through her attorney.

Some divorcees mistakenly assume that the divorce court, on its own, somehow monitors compliance with orders it has issued. It does not. The court that handled your divorce has neither the resources nor the authority to do so. If there is any noncompliance with a court order issued in your case, *you* must be the one to take action. Likewise, your divorce attorney is unable to monitor compliance because their representation of you presumably ended when the divorce was finalized. Consequently, noncompliance is a post-decree matter that must be brought to your attorney's attention, and as a new matter, it will probably require a new representation agreement and retainer.

In Angela's case, it was up to her to file a motion to hold Andy in contempt for his violation of the divorce decree and to enforce the court order to ensure that the house was listed for sale. Instead, Angela's inattentiveness and inaction left her with a mess on her hands that will take more of her time and cost her more money to clean up. It will also hamper Angela's ability to buy a house of her own anytime soon because she will be seen by other lenders as already being financially obligated on another mortgage. With each mortgage payment Andy misses, Angela's credit score takes a hit. Now, with a damaged credit score due to Andy's missed payments, a pending foreclosure lawsuit on her record, and her name still on the home loan, Angela has virtually no chance of securing a home loan in her name anytime soon.

Example 2—Joint Car Loan:

In the divorce between Ron and Tammy, the court determined that Tammy could keep the Honda Pilot that was secured by a joint loan in both of their names to Capital One Auto Finance. The divorce decree ordered Ron to transfer ownership solely to Tammy, and it allocated Tammy 60 days to obtain refinancing on the vehicle or pay off the balance. If she was unable to obtain refinancing or to extinguish the debt by full payment to Capital One, Tammy was required to sell the vehicle so as to terminate Ron's responsibility on the debt. Tammy was also ordered to maintain automobile insurance on the vehicle through the date of sale or refinancing. The decree further provided that if the vehicle was sold, Tammy was entitled to receive any profits from the sale of the vehicle but would be solely responsible for any deficiency in the event the proceeds were insufficient to cover the balance of the debt. In addition, she was ordered to make the car payments pending refinancing or the sale of the vehicle.

Ron failed to transfer his ownership interest in the Pilot and didn't keep tabs on Tammy's refinancing of the car loan. He also stopped making the car insurance payments because he believed that Tammy would comply with the court's order that she be responsible for the insurance payments. Tammy never made the payments, and the coverage lapsed.

Ninety days passed after the divorce decree was filed, and Tammy not only failed to refinance the vehicle but also started missing her car payments. Tammy made one car payment but missed the following two. Capital One Auto Finance contacted Ron by phone after the second missed payment. Ron then called Tammy, and she assured him that it was just a misunderstanding with the lender and that the check was in the mail. It was not.

Another 30 days went by, and Tammy missed another car payment. Ron got a call from the lender asking for the location of the car so it could be repossessed. He was shocked that Tammy had once again missed the car payment and was furious that she had lied to him. After all, money had always been an issue of contention during their marriage.

When Ron called Tammy to tell her that he gave the lender her new address so they could repossess the Pilot, she told Ron that she had been in a car accident the day before and that it was totaled. She admitted to Ron that she ran a red light and struck another vehicle, injuring its driver and passengers. The cops wrote her a citation, finding her to be at fault. One officer on the scene told Tammy, "I hope you have good car insurance and an even better lawyer."

Just like Angela in Example 1, Ron has a certifiable mess on his hands as a result of his inaction and failure to closely monitor Tammy's compliance with the court order. Since Ron is a titled owner of the vehicle, he should expect to be named as a defendant in any personal injury lawsuit. Even worse, since Tammy never obtained insurance on the vehicle after his insurance lapsed, Ron could have significant financial exposure in the lawsuit. This illustration, albeit extreme, should be a wake-up call to you and a reminder to be vigilant. This type of stuff actually happens.

Ron made at least three mistakes. First, he should have immediately taken steps to transfer his ownership interest in the vehicle solely into Tammy's name. Second, he should have ensured that the vehicle was covered by his insurance until it was transferred out of his name, in addition to making the payments on the insurance just to protect himself even if Tammy had violated the court order. Finally, Ron should have enforced the terms of the divorce decree by filing a contempt motion with the court to demand the car be handed over to him so he could sell it and seek reimbursement for any car loan and insurance payments he had to make due to Tammy's failures to comply with the court order.

Ron is not going to be able to defend himself in the personal injury lawsuit by simply pointing to the divorce decree. He was a titled owner of the uninsured vehicle at the time of the accident. Similarly, Ron cannot use the divorce decree as a defense when he is sued by Capital One for the balance of the car loan since he is still an obligor on the loan. In other words, Ron could be up a creek. This is all to say that while your divorce decree may be the final filing in your divorce action, it is merely an enforceable court order that allocates assets and debts. It does not replace legal titles or deeds, nor does it wipe clean promissory notes and loans in your name simply because it orders your ex-spouse to be responsible for a debt. You must be the one to monitor compliance and enforce the court order.

Example 3—Credit Card Debt:

In Donna and Joe's divorce decree, Joe was ordered to be solely responsible for extinguishing the $5,000 of credit card debt that was on a Home Depot credit card issued only in Donna's name. The divorce decree *ordered Joe to make minimum payments of at least $500 per month and required him to pay off the entire card balance, including interest, within six months.*

Donna, who was a coworker of Angela's (Example 1) and Ron's (Example 2), knew of the importance of keeping tabs on Joe's payments post-divorce thanks to their respective cautionary tales. So, Donna checked the balance of her Home Depot credit card every week to ensure that Joe was making payments per the divorce decree.

Joe made timely payments for the first two months, but he only paid $250 in the third month. Donna immediately sent him an email indicating that he had 48 hours to pay the other $250 he owed, or she was filing a contempt motion with the court. He complied.

At the end of six months, Joe had paid off $3,000 in principal because he had made payments of $500 each month for six months, but he had not eliminated the remaining $2,000 balance and $700 of interest that had accrued. Donna emailed Joe and informed him that if the balance was not paid off in a week, she was taking him back to court. Joe did not acknowledge her email, nor did he pay off the balance. So, Donna contacted and retained an attorney to take the necessary steps to enforce the court order.

Donna's attorney filed a motion to show cause, and the court set a hearing on Donna's claim that Joe was in contempt. The court found Joe in contempt, ordered him to pay off the balance in 30 days, and awarded Donna her attorney's fees and the court costs involved with bringing the motion.

Again, Joe failed to pay off the balance, so the court set another hearing date after Donna reported Joe's noncompliance. This time, the court sentenced Joe to a weekend in jail and issued a withholding order to Joe's employer in the amount of the outstanding debt, attorney's fees, and court costs.

In this example, Donna did exactly what she was supposed to do. She knew exactly what was required of Joe because she knew the terms of her divorce decree. Donna kept tabs on Joe, and she held him accountable when he was noncompliant with the terms of the decree. Fortunately, Donna was able to learn from the mistakes of Angela and Ron. Be like Donna.

I am astonished by the number of phone calls I get from people like Angela and Ron, seeking the help of an attorney long after the damage is already done and things have completely spiraled out of control. Your life will be much easier if you act early. To do so, you must know precisely what is ordered by the court in your divorce decree, and you must hold your ex-spouse accountable as soon as it becomes necessary—especially if your name is on a debt that they are ordered to pay.

Technology allows you to monitor your ex-spouse's compliance—or lack thereof—easier than ever before. Calendar the obligations on your smartphone and computer. If their deadline to pay off a debt or refinance debt in your name has passed, act right away, either on your own or with the help of an attorney. Send an email or text message to remind your ex of their obligation. Oversights certainly happen. If it turns out not to be an oversight, then threaten, in writing, to take legal action. Inaction is not an option, as illustrated in the cases of Angela and Ron, because nonpayment of your debt can have long-lasting adverse consequences on your financial recovery. I hope that you can learn from all three of these illustrations and will take the next opportunity you have to reread your divorce decree to ensure you are familiar with its terms.

Do establish post-divorce boundaries; don't be an enabler.

Divorcees who have no children with their ex-spouse can start the next chapter of their lives without being tied to their former partner. Once the financial entanglements are unwound, there is unlikely to be any communication between exes, and therefore there is no apparent need to establish post-divorce boundaries.

However, if you have children with your ex-spouse, the two of you will be inextricably linked for the rest of your lives. Whether you realize it or not, you and your ex-spouse will have to coexist with each other until the day you die. Your children are going to grow up, graduate from school, get married, and, presumably, have your grandchildren. Some parents can work together after divorce without any major battles. Others are so combative that drama is nearly guaranteed at their offspring's biggest life events. Divorced parents have been known to cause a scene at college graduations, weddings, and other notable family events, including at the hospital while their first grandchild is being delivered. This type of tension doesn't just play out in the movies. Many of us have attended weddings before where there was concern about the bride or groom's divorced parents making a scene. Don't let that be you.

Given the lifetime connection that you will have with your ex-spouse by virtue of your children, it is important to establish boundaries the moment your divorce is finalized. Regardless of how amicable or not you and your ex-spouse are, you will get requests (or demands) from them regarding parenting time and child-related expenses. The reason boundaries are important in your post-divorce financial recovery is that your former partner may constantly try to squeeze time and money out of you by using the children as a pretext for both.

There is no one-size-fits-all solution anyone can offer to address the idiosyncrasies of your ex-spouse. Yet, without question, the best resource for guidance on setting limits is the aptly named book *Boundaries: When to Say Yes, How to Say No to Take Control of Your Life* by Dr. Henry Cloud and Dr. John Townsend. This book will teach you how to establish boundaries, recognize chronic boundary violators, and handle people in your life who constantly violate them. It will also educate you on how to identify the techniques frequent violators employ to try to sidestep the boundaries you put in place.

> *A lack of planning on your part doesn't constitute an emergency on my part.*
> **– Coffee Mug Quote**

When it comes to parenting time, your ex-spouse may constantly ask for modifications to the established schedule to accommodate their plans. You must be able to distinguish between a one-off request (or demand) and a sign of things to come. There is certainly a difference between your ex-spouse asking to swap weekends because of their grandparent's birthday falling on your delineated weekend and your ex making such requests a dozen times a year because *all* of their extended family celebrations curiously seem to fall on *your* weekends.

Your ability to establish boundaries starts with the terms of your divorce decree. Your familiarity with the court order will allow you to recognize whether a request (or demand) from your former partner requires your compliance under the terms of the decree or if it is beyond what is legally required of you. Conversely, if you are unfamiliar with the terms of the decree, you will not be able to distinguish the difference, and you might find yourself being taken advantage of by your ex-spouse.

Many post-divorce conflicts arise from what is *not* in the court's order.

The benefit of a clearly worded divorce decree is that there is no question about who is responsible for a particular expense. Generic, ambiguous, and poorly worded decrees lead to confusion, conflict, and avoidance of responsibility. Child support—and, more specifically, the responsibility for child-related expenses—tends to be fertile ground for disputes.

Since child support law varies from state to state, there is no universal guidance that applies to every case. Certainly, the best place to start is your divorce decree, or whichever court order in your case addresses child support and child-related expenses. Your decree may spell out your obligation in plain and simple language for you to point to in the event of a dispute. For instance, if the decree states that you are responsible for paying child support and specific, delineated child-related expenses (such as a percentage of the child's uninsured medical expenses) but nothing beyond those expenses, then your obligation is (fortunately) spelled out for you in black and white. If your decree is not so clear, however, and there are gray areas around child-related expenses, you have a recipe for contention between you and your ex-spouse regarding who is responsible for which expense. You may need to seek legal advice or reopen the case to clarify any confusion.

Nevertheless, even with a crystal-clear decree that spells out child support in detail and identifies the precise responsibilities of each parent regarding child-related expenses, conflict can still arise from both sides. Let's look at examples of each:

Example 1—The Parent Ordered to Pay Does Not Pay:

If the parent who is ordered to be the payor of child support (also known as the obligor), plus a set percentage of uninsured medical expenses, fails to pay under the terms of the court order, the support-receiving parent (also known as the obligee) must determine whether they are going to tolerate the noncompliance. In most jurisdictions, the state will make an effort of its own accord to prosecute delinquent obligors. The more common issue that divorcees encounter is their former partner not paying for court-ordered medical expenses or some other extracurricular expense that is specifically ordered in the decree.

If you accept or ignore your ex-spouse's noncompliance, meaning you tacitly consent to their behavior, then you establish a precedent that they do not have to pay you money that they owe to you. Your ex-spouse may convince you not to take any action by saying things like: "*I don't have the money,*" "*I don't care what the court says since I'm not going to pay you back, ever,*" or "*Take me to court if you have to because nothing is going to happen anyway.*" If these excuses and threats are effective and you don't act, you will have set a bad precedent. From that point onward, you can expect no change in your ex-spouse's behavior because you have given the green light to disobey the court order.

I certainly understand that post-decree contempt motions are a pain, but nonpayment by your ex-spouse slows down your financial recovery. Every dollar you are owed that you choose not to make any effort to collect is a dollar that could be applied to your debt, children's college fund, retirement, and mortgage. Those dollars add up over time. Your progress will lag if you choose not to hold your former partner accountable. Ask yourself:

Do I want to delay my retirement because I'm not willing to stand up for myself and enforce the court order so I can get paid the money my ex-spouse owes me?

Your answer should be "*NO!*" Additionally, the cost to you of allowing noncompliance is not just financial but also emotional, as anger will build up inside of you every time it happens. If your ex-spouse pulls up to your house in a new car, posts pictures on Facebook of their latest vacation, or flaunts some frivolous new purchase at your child's soccer game—all while owing you hundreds or even thousands of dollars—you might blow a gasket. So, if you find yourself in such a situation, now is the time to get legal advice or even initiate the contempt action on your own. It is also the perfect time to reexamine the boundaries you have put in place with your ex-spouse.

Example 2—The Parent Receiving the Child Support is Irresponsible with Money:

Just as common as the non-paying parent is the situation where the support-receiving parent is completely irresponsible with the money they receive. All too frequently, I meet with people who are paying their court-ordered child support plus a significant amount in expenses they are not legally obligated to pay because their ex-spouse is either (1) irresponsible handling money or (2) manipulative and therefore able to extract additional payments. Sometimes it is both. In my experience, if you are facing one or both of these situations, you probably have boundaries and enabling issues.

Every year, I see at least one or two extreme examples where the child-support-receiving parent who is responsible for the child's expenses, including buying the clothes, tells the support-paying parent that they do not have money to buy the child's necessities. The conversation looks something like this:

I know you pay me child support, but I cannot afford to buy our son a winter coat. If you think that he needs a winter coat, you buy it! I don't have the money! I can't help that it's 28 degrees outside. What, are you too cheap to buy your son a coat?

Then the paying parent is left with what seems to be a dire decision: either buy the coat or take the chance that their child may freeze because the other parent may be crazy enough to send the child out to the bus stop without a coat.

If you find yourself in this type of situation and you give in, you will have established the precedent that even though you are doing what is legally obligated of you—in this example, paying child support—your ex-spouse does not need to budget or spend the money they receive to cover your child's most basic needs.

You will have also signaled your willingness to be the new go-to source of funds—the ATM, if you will—that can be tapped whenever your ex can use your "child's needs" as a means of manipulation. Your ex will have learned that if they take an absurd, indefensible position (e.g., it is *impossible* for them to scrape together the money to buy a coat for your child in the middle of winter, even from a thrift store), you will give in and pay up. Additionally, you will have enabled their bad behavior, regardless if it was intentionally vindictive on their part or simply due to their chronic irresponsibility with money. Why should your ex-spouse act responsibly with money when everyone knows that *you* will be there to bail them out so long as their request is veiled as fulfilling your child's basic needs?

You may be thinking: "*Whatever. If my kid needs a coat, I'm buying him a coat. I don't care if I'm ordered to pay it or not. I'm a good parent, and my kid's needs come first.*" That is a perfectly rational response and one that I hear all the time. Based on my experience, if you allow your ex-spouse to hold your child's safety hostage with the excuse, *"I don't have the money, so if you don't pay for it, your child will be in danger of* [fill in the dangerous situation]," you are likely an enabler, especially if your ex knows that you will eventually break down and pony up because you don't want to be labeled a "bad parent."

If you look back at your past responses to your ex-spouse's behavior and you realize that you have been an enabler all along, now is the time to change. Seek out professional guidance if you need additional advice outside of what is offered in the book *Boundaries*. A therapist can help you learn how to create limits, recognize manipulative tactics used by your ex-spouse, and curtail your enabling when these situations arise.

> *You get what you tolerate.*
>
> **– Dr. Henry Cloud**

While recognizing and ceasing enabling behavior may be easier said than done, know that the noble cause of providing for your children will have no bounds, especially if your ex-spouse comes to realize that you will eventually pay. Once your ex knows that you will break down and be the one to buy the winter coat, there is no need on their part to budget for the cost of that coat anymore. Your child support payment goes to the same account as their paycheck and other sources of income. If they have the money to dine out, go to the movies, travel, or buy any non-essential *want*, they certainly have the money to buy their child a coat. By allowing your ex-spouse to continue to be irresponsible with money, and until you change how you respond, these kinds of situations will inevitably continue to occur.

Unfortunately, your child is stuck in the middle. Your act of drawing a line in the sand may mean your ex-spouse follows through on the threat and sends your child out to the bus stop in freezing temperatures without a coat. If you are dealing with this type of person, my heart goes out to you. You and your attorney will need to figure out how you are going to handle this situation and obtain sole custody. There is no simple answer or technique that I can teach you to deal with such outrageous behavior. Understandably, the last thing you want to see is your child suffer.

Yet, *you* will assuredly financially suffer if you allow yourself to be taken advantage of by your ex-spouse in any manner. If you do not establish boundaries and check your enabling behavior, your bank account will be bled dry by your parasitic ex. When you think of every dollar swindled out of you specifically as a dollar that you could have otherwise applied to your debt, your child's college fund, retirement, and financial recovery, you should be fired up to the point that you take action. Consider the impact that your inaction has on your child's future. Do you want your child's college fund to be barren at age 18 because the money you originally intended to deposit there was instead diverted to your ex-spouse due to their irresponsibility and self-serving, manipulative behavior? I'd bet that you do not.

This is a difficult topic for me to explain and presumably for you to digest because manipulators are very clever in their tactics. This discussion is important because boundaries are crucial in your life post-divorce because they are necessary to protect yourself financially. If your ex-spouse was horrible with money while you were married, it is unrealistic to expect that same person to magically become financially responsible after divorce. If your ex-spouse was manipulative during the marriage, I would expect it to only get worse after the divorce.

If your ex-spouse continues to struggle with money, there is nothing you can do to change their behavior. The only thing you can control is *your* conduct, which includes your responses to their requests and demands. My best guidance is: know your obligations, stick to your principles, establish limits, and do not enable bad behavior. You are not your ex-spouse's keeper, ATM, or parent—nor should you be.

———————◖◗———————

Update your will and beneficiary forms, and make sure the retirement division orders are prepared and filed.

Immediately after your divorce is finalized, you should update the beneficiary forms on all of your financial accounts, retirement accounts, and life insurance policy. You should also update your will.[15] You may be focused on other things, but most beneficiary forms are available online and will take a minute of your time to fill out. In the event of your untimely death, do you want the proceeds of your life insurance policy to go to your ex-spouse? I didn't think so.

Also, you may see the phrase "Qualified Domestic Relations Order" or "Division of Property Order" in your divorce decree with regard to the division of retirement accounts and pensions. While your divorce decree may order a retirement account or pension to be divided, that order has no effect unless the corresponding legal document—e.g., a Qualified Domestic Relations Order ("QDRO") in the event of a private company's 401k or pension plan; a Division of Property Order ("DOPO") in the event of a public pension plan—is prepared, filed with the court, and sent to the plan administrator. Every month or so, my office gets a call from a divorcee whose case was closed more than 20 years ago, but no QDRO or DOPO was ever prepared.

---

15. If you do not have a will or medical power of attorney, you must make it a priority to get those documents done. Each state has different requirements, so see a local attorney or use a legal forms website. It is a straightforward and painless process, and simple estate planning done by an experienced attorney tends to be less expensive than you would think.

Because of that, they are not able to receive any of their ex-spouse's retirement funds to which they are entitled. If you try to address this in a decade instead of right now, it can cost you a significant amount in lost benefits and attorney's fees. Make sure you finalize the transfer of retirement funds by having your attorney prepare the QDRO or DOPO documents necessary to accomplish this task.

Finally, while you are at it, update your income tax withholdings with your employer's HR representative. Your tax withholdings have likely been based upon your household's income while married. So, to avoid a surprise tax obligation in April, update your withholdings now.

Mistake #5:

Making Poor Financial Decisions When Your Melodramatic Alter Ego Takes Over

———●———

Each of us has an inner five-year-old. There are times when we want something so badly that the overly dramatic five-year-old inside of us acts out, just like the child at the grocery store who throws a temper tantrum because his mom said no to the sugar-filled cereal he so desperately wants. You've seen this play out so many times it's easy to picture that kid. His face turns red, his emotions take over, and he screams and cries that his life is over unless he gets what he wants. Despite all the years that have passed since any of us last threw a fit in public, we are still capable of behaving in a way that is fueled by that same level of emotion. As adults, it comes in the form of—for lack of a better descriptive phrase—our "Melodramatic Alter Ego." The difference between the adult and the child versions of this behavior is that we, as adults, are able to disguise that emotional response with justifications and mental gymnastics.

The biggest mistakes I have made with money, and the biggest mistakes I have observed others make with money—divorcees included—occur when we give in to that Melodramatic Alter Ego. Adults do a better job of hiding it than children do. We use some honorable, higher calling as our excuse for making a purchase that is fueled by the emotions of our Melodramatic Alter Ego—not the rational part of our brains.

For divorcees, the justification is cloaked as a higher calling and appears in various forms. Keeping the overly-expensive marital home "so my children's lives won't be interrupted," buying a brand-new $40,000 SUV "because I want my kids to be safe," or constantly engaging in retail therapy "because I just want to be happy" are all pretext for rationalizing damaging behavior.

The problem is that when we are in Melodramatic Alter Ego mode, we box ourselves into two possible decisions with money. The first is the one where the noble purpose is served—it takes care of your child; it brings you short-term happiness after months of sorrow; it eases your pain; etc. The second possible decision is only focused on money. When we limit ourselves to just two choices, we create a false dichotomy that says *"the only way to not choose money over my family is to go through with this irresponsible financial decision."*

A former client of mine, immediately after her divorce was finalized, sold her paid-off Honda Accord for $5,000 and bought a brand-new $40,000 SUV. She looked me directly in the eyes and said that she was *forced* to buy the SUV for the well-being of her children because they were not safe in the Honda Accord. She explained that there were no issues with the Honda Accord, outside of the fact that it was 12 years old and did not have the automatic emergency braking feature that her brand-new SUV had. The SUV also had a $550 monthly loan payment and a higher insurance rate than the Honda Accord. The purchase was substantial compared to her annual salary of $50,000, but she believed it was the best move she could make for her family's safety.

In reality, she had boxed herself into the mindset that her paid-off vehicle was no longer safe, and there were not any other acceptable solutions to satisfy the apparent nobility of ensuring her children's safety besides buying this brand-new $40,000 SUV. Although she was not stomping her feet and screaming at the top of her lungs in the cereal aisle, the Melodramatic Alter Ego inside of her had certainly taken over. It led her to make an ill-advised financial decision that she is likely still dealing with to this day.

If you find yourself trying to justify a financial choice because you feel forced to do it based on a higher calling (e.g., "for the good of my children!"), you are headed toward the cliff of making a bad decision. Simply put, you are about to give in to your Melodramatic Alter Ego, who has you boxed-in. Even worse, whenever that version of you wins out, your financial recovery takes longer and longer to achieve because you tie up more of your money paying for it.

One of the most common underwater assets in divorces is the RV camper. Typically, campers are purchased during the marriage with the idea that it will facilitate cross-country traveling and thus create positive experiences for both the parents and their children. Yet, campers lose their value at an incredible rate, much faster than even a brand-new vehicle.

On too many occasions to count, I have had clients insist on keeping the RV and the debt associated with it because they believed it would generate happy memories for the kids, offsetting whatever pain they had experienced during the divorce. Wanting to create positive memories for your children is certainly a noble calling—but taking on a substantial amount of debt on an underwater RV and having to work overtime that takes you away from your kids just to afford the payments defeats the goal.

Are children important? Absolutely. Is their safety important? Absolutely. Is your time with them important? Absolutely. Is your happiness post-divorce important? Absolutely. I am not saying these are not noble callings or worthy reasons because they certainly are that.

Your decision-making paradigm breaks down when you start giving into the part of your brain that puts the noble calling above all else, regardless of the financial cost, as if there are *only* two options in front of you. The Melodramatic Alter Ego makes you think: *"I am forced to buy this $40,000 SUV; otherwise, my kids aren't going to be safe!"* or *"I had to keep the house because the kids needed that part of their life to stay the same!"* or *"Without the $60,000 RV, my kids and I will not be able to create amazing memories together!"*

My response is:

Maybe not.

Maybe there's another way to solve this problem.

Maybe I do not have to buy a $40,000 SUV for my children to be safe in a vehicle.

Maybe I can rent an apartment for 18 months until my debt is cleaned up.

Maybe I do not have to pay $60,000 for an RV so I can enjoy time with my children while they are in my care.

Maybe my children and I can make fond memories together that do not require taking on more debt at the expense of their college education and my retirement account.

Maybe I can start searching for some other options besides the two that my Melodramatic Alter Ego has given me.

Maybe there is another option out there besides Option A (which is good for the children, my happiness, etc. but financially stupid) and Option B (which abandons the noble cause but is financially smart).

These are not just maybes; they are realities.

If you box yourself into a false dichotomy, which your Melodramatic Alter Ego often does, you will inherently make unwise financial decisions, time and time again. Moreover, whenever this happens, it will set you back financially for years. One imprudent financial decision does more harm to your family in the long run, well beyond what you were trying to protect them from in the first place. If you have to spend more hours at work to pay for the financial choices you've made that were fueled by your Melodramatic Alter Ego, your family is not better off. Keeping the marital home for the sake of your children, while premised upon a noble intent, will not benefit them if they never see you because you have to constantly work overtime just to make the mortgage payment.

If you are reading this and think the message is to *choose money over my children and happiness*, you are mistaken. My point is that you cannot allow yourself to be limited to only two choices that include just the noble calling *or* the money. The Melodramatic Alter Ego prevails when you box yourself in like that, and you end up paying dearly for it. There is almost always a third option—which is *Option C: None of the above*. Find another way to cross the river. You are fully capable of finding another way to make a decision that best serves you, your family, *and* your financial recovery. Option C may slow down your financial progress, but it avoids you giving in to that five-year-old with the red face, screaming at the top of his lungs in the grocery store.

Giving in to your Melodramatic Alter Ego will lead you to make major financial decisions that are 100% guaranteed to stall your post-divorce financial recovery. You must resist it at all costs. I get that this is easier said than done, but it is of paramount importance in light of your goals and the journey you are on. I see this play out all the time in divorce cases themselves.

Litigants who want to fight over every single item, just because they are angry at their soon-to-be ex-spouse, pay exponentially more to their attorneys because their emotions have taken over.

I regularly tell my clients that it makes no sense to pay my hourly rate for items that can easily be replaced for a fraction of the cost. Not all attorneys are so forthright. Many are more than happy to take your money when you want to fight over the "principle" of something. Paying tens of thousands of dollars to pick a fight because you are mad at your soon-to-be ex-spouse is a tell-tale sign that the Melodramatic Alter Ego inside of you has taken hostage the rational part of your brain.

Divorce courts are not in the business of telling your ex-spouse that they are a "bad person;" the court's job is to divide assets and debts, dole out custody and support orders, and legally terminate the marriage. I see the most money spent on custody fights when the issues between the ex-spouses are of nominal concern to the court. Attorneys across the country are collectively paid millions of dollars every year by litigants who are hellbent on preventing their ex-spouses from having a couple more overnight visits with the kids every month. Maybe there is another way to handle disputes with your ex-spouse without draining your bank account and sabotaging your financial recovery.

Acknowledging the existence of your Melodramatic Alter Ego is particularly important for divorcees, who can easily find themselves rationalizing major financial decisions for the sake of their personal and family happiness, safety, stability, and overall well-being after a disruptive and emotionally-draining divorce. Buying an expensive new car outside your price range and claiming it's the only option available on the market that will ensure your children can travel to soccer practice safely will wreck your financial recovery. Refusing to part with the marital residence that you cannot afford to "make things easier for the children" will put you in a financial hole and keep you there for years. Virtually every purchase you make, big and small, can be cloaked in some sort of rationale that leads you to believe it is the only acceptable decision.

Since your world was recently rocked by a divorce, there are going to be numerous possible justifications you can pick from and choose to use; any of these excuses will serve as a basis to make bad decision after bad decision. And your support network will struggle to convince you otherwise as long as you have decided to commit yourself to only two possible paths—spend the money to achieve the nobility or totally sacrifice the nobility because money is more important.

In your situation, you have to be strong enough to ignore the inner voice that urgently says, "*Go ahead and buy this! After everything you've been through this past year, you deserve it. You deserve to be happy!*" You must avoid overextending yourself by buying things beyond your budget and paying for experiences you cannot afford for some higher purpose that you have identified as being of paramount importance in your life. The realities of your post-divorce financial situation are the exact reason why you cannot give in to these justifications that are all fueled by that Melodramatic Alter Ego inside of you.

Deep down, you know that your children will be just fine if they have to share a bedroom, move with you to a new residence, wear sneakers that aren't the newest Nike's, be safe with you in a vehicle that was manufactured before 2016, and experience less luxurious vacations than you took while married. When you're not filled with emotion, the rational side of you recognizes that your kids will still live a good life even if you have to move to a smaller residence and buy them clothes from more economical stores than in the past. I know the Melodramatic Alter Ego inside of you screams otherwise, claiming that there is no middle ground and that to truly make your children safe it will require that $40,000 SUV since *no other option* will suffice. Yet, in almost every situation imaginable, a third option exists beyond the two created in your false dichotomy.

Look at it this way: it is actually a noble calling to take care of your children by getting your financial affairs in order, in addition to assisting in paying for their college education. It is also admirable to be in the position to be able to save for your retirement now so you are not a burden on your kids when you are 70 years old. If you constantly give in to your Melodramatic Alter Ego, you will find your children's college fund barren and your retirement account underfunded, maybe even empty. This would be the opposite of nobility, as you would have failed to be a good manager of the money you earned over the rest of your working life.

> *Children do what feels good.*
> *Adults devise a plan and follow it.*
> **– Dave Ramsey**

When you find yourself faced with making a major financial decision, determine whether you are being influenced by your Melodramatic Alter Ego or not. If the item you have twisted yourself into thinking unquestionably of as a *need* is actually a *want*, it's a good sign that the five-year-old melting down in the cereal aisle has taken over.

Mistake #6:

Listening to Broke People, Enablers, and "Hype Men"

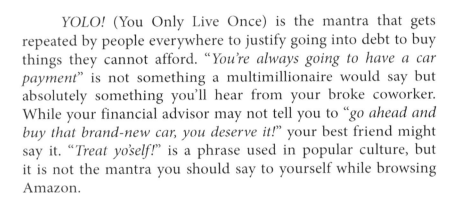

YOLO! (You Only Live Once) is the mantra that gets repeated by people everywhere to justify going into debt to buy things they cannot afford. *"You're always going to have a car payment"* is not something a multimillionaire would say but absolutely something you'll hear from your broke coworker. While your financial advisor may not tell you to *"go ahead and buy that brand-new car, you deserve it!"* your best friend might say it. *"Treat yo'self!"* is a phrase used in popular culture, but it is not the mantra you should say to yourself while browsing Amazon.

While I am in favor of your friends, family members, and coworkers walking alongside you in your financial recovery journey and giving you feedback along the way, there are some people whose advice you simply must ignore. The same way you would not ask for health tips from the least healthy person you know, you should not take financial advice from people who are broke. Unfortunately, you know a ton of broke people. Even worse, many of them do not think of themselves as financially unwise, even though their bank accounts, credit card bills, and net worth say otherwise. Statistically, many of your close friends and acquaintances have car payments, credit card debt, a mortgage, and not much saved for emergencies.

The *Report on the Economic Well-Being of U.S. Households in 2018*, an ongoing study conducted by the Federal Reserve that began in 2013, found that one-third of Americans would be forced into a difficult financial situation if they faced an unexpected expense of just $400. The same study revealed that 25% of Americans had nothing saved for retirement, and the collective amount of student loan debt for Americans exceeded $1.5 trillion. In addition, more than 70% of Americans live paycheck to paycheck, including 25% of households with an income of $150,000 or more.[16] So what does all of this mean for you? You are surrounded by people who do not have their financial act together, who have no problem taking on and using debt, who are bad stewards with their own money, and whose input you should ignore when it comes to *your* finances.

While some people you know and love are holding their tongues because they are hesitant to talk to you about your spending, lifestyle, and retail therapy, there are plenty of others in your life who have no problem spouting off mantras about how you should "live for today" and spend your money now because "you could get hit by a truck tomorrow."[17] The bottom line is that you cannot take your financial advice from people who don't know how to manage their money. If someone does not share the same outlook as you when it comes to debt, savings, and investing, do not waste your time talking to them about anything to do with personal finance. Instead, talk about *literally anything else* with them—just not your finances.

If you want to become rich, do what rich people do. That means paying for things with money you have and living within your means. If you are curious as to what rich people do, the

---

16. Nicole Lyn Pesce, *A Shocking Number of Americans Are Living Paycheck to Paycheck*, MARKETWATCH (Jan. 11, 2020), https://www.marketwatch.com/story/a-shocking-number-of-americans-are-living-paycheck-to-paycheck-2020-01-07.
17. A friend of mine from college actually did get hit by a truck and lived to tell the story. *How to Get Run Over by a Truck*, a memoir by Katie McKenna, is one of the most inspirational books I have ever read. Add it to your reading list. It will certainly help put things in perspective for you as you handle the problems in your life. It will also make you laugh, cry, and be motivated to seize the day.

perfect place to start is the best-selling book *The Millionaire Next Door: The Surprising Secrets of America's Wealthy* by Dr. Thomas Stanley and Dr. William Danko. This book describes in detail the spending and savings habits of typical millionaires, who exist in large numbers in your community but do not act or behave like the millionaire celebrities and athletes we see on television.

When most people hear the word "millionaire," they think of rich and famous athletes, rock stars, foreign oligarchs, business tycoons, and trust-fund recipients who inherited all their wealth. *The Millionaire Next Door* dispels these and other myths about millionaires and instead reveals that the majority of millionaires in the U.S. are first-generation wealthy—meaning they did not inherit their money.

On average, millionaires' spending habits are not lavish, as what they spend on blue jeans, suits, and even restaurants pale in comparison to what most people spend on the same things. According to Dr. Stanley's research, the typical millionaire buys reliable, used vehicles, on average two years old, because the depreciation during the first two years is the greatest and therefore borne by someone else. His research also shows that the average millionaire does not live in a McMansion or flaunt signs of wealth. The book paints the picture of modest, generous, non-flashy lifestyles of people whose friends and family are often clueless as to their wealth.

The Millionaire Next Door is required reading for you, as it tells you precisely what spending habits you should adopt in your life if you want to achieve wealth. Once you read the book, you will look at your spending differently, and it will help you escape the trap of listening to your broke friends, family members, and coworkers when they inevitably try to give you advice on your finances and spending habits.

The 60-, 70-, and 80-year-olds who are busy spending their golden years driving luxury automobiles, traveling the world, sailing on cruise ships, flying first-class, and living lavish lifestyles are not funding their travels on the minuscule social security check they receive each month. Your coworker who just bought a brand-new truck, financed at 14.99% interest because his credit is awful and who has nothing saved for retirement, is just like the chain-smoking stranger at the bar who just survived his 5th heart attack trying to give you tips on how to stay healthy.

Soon enough, you will be living on a budget, making sacrifices, and seeing progress in paying down debt and building up your savings and retirement funds. You will say the word "no" to invitations quite frequently during this time when you are digging out of debt. You'll decline requests to dinners, concerts, sporting events, and getaways, and in return you will likely be met with resistance. "*Come on! You deserve a night out!*" may be the closing argument of someone who simply does not understand your financial journey.

You cannot become debt-free—and, more importantly, stay debt-free—unless you have discipline, frugal habits, and the ability to say no to big and small temptations. What would your budget look like if every month you had *no* mortgage payment, car payment, credit card payment, student loan payment, or loan payment? You would have money build up each and every month. You would have the ability to save, invest, and build wealth at such an incredible rate you would eventually be in a position to be financially independent. That's our ultimate goal.

My first goal for you is to be *totally* debt-free. For you to get there, you need to do what other debt-free people do. The good financial influences in your life right now are probably few and far between. That said, there is a community of others just like you. They are working on getting out of debt, saving intently for their retirements, and becoming completely debt-free. In Part II of this book, I am going to show you where to find them.

"Hype men" exist outside of entertainer and pro-athlete entourages.

I am a longtime fan of professional boxing. I love watching the entrances of the fighters as they walk from the dressing room to the ring because the theatrics remind me of the pro-wrestling I used to watch as a kid. The most notable difference between the two is that pro-wrestlers typically walk to the ring by themselves, while boxers always have an entourage that accompanies them. Sometimes it is just the trainer and the cutman, but for bigger fights, the entourage can be a dozen people or more.

Professional boxing is a mess of a sport from an organizational level[18] because there are many sanctioning bodies—collectively known as the "alphabet soup" (WBC, WBO, WBA, IBF, etc.)—that each have their own champions and belts. It is common for a boxer to have five or six championship belts from each of the various sanctioning bodies. It is also a standard practice for each belt to be hoisted by a member of the entourage as the champ walks to the ring to the crowd's thunderous applause. It is a spectacle that I always enjoy.[19] This is one example of a "hype man."

---

18. I wrote an article about the problems plaguing professional boxing in 2006. Unfortunately for the sport, little has changed since then. *See* Michael J. Jurek, *Janitor or Savior: The Role of Congress in Professional Boxing Reform*, 67 Ohio St. L.J. 1187 (2006).
19. It is a dream of mine to be a member of a fighter's entourage where my job is to do nothing more than carry a belt over my head and walk to the ring behind the fighter, with eight others doing the same thing, just to hype up the crowd and remind the fighter that he is the champ.

While not defined by the Cambridge Dictionary, Wikipedia nonetheless describes a hype man as someone who "in hip hop music and rapping is a backup rapper or singer who supports the primary rappers with exclamations and interjections and who attempts to increase the audience's excitement with call-and-response chants."[20] Flavor Flav and Lil Jon are among the most recognizable hype men in popular culture; even non-fans of rap would likely recognize their names.

For lack of a better descriptive phrase, I think hype man is an appropriate term to use for someone in your life who not only has your ear but also has a unique way of getting you fired up about something in your life. The hype man is not always an enabler because they are not necessarily financing the bad behavior, but rather they offer suggestive advice that has the impact of instigating an emotional response. I see this happen all the time in divorce cases and post-decree custody disputes.

In almost every case I handle, my client has received both solicited and unsolicited advice from their well-meaning, non-attorney friends and family members on what to do in their divorce case. If you tell people in your life that you have a legal issue, some of your non-attorney acquaintances will have no problem spouting off "street advice" about how you should handle the situation. Since divorce is so prevalent, almost everyone knows someone who has already been through it.

I always raise an eyebrow whenever I hear about someone getting "screwed" in a divorce because the law tends to be clear about the equitable division of property, and as such, it is one of the most predictable areas of law to practice. Within the first 15 minutes of meeting a prospective client, I should have a good idea based on the facts of the case whether spousal support will

---

20. *Hype Men*, WIKIPEDIA, https://en.wikipedia.org/wiki/Hype_man (last visited October 4, 2020).

be an issue, the likelihood of resolving the case based on the outstanding issues, and how the assets and debts of the marriage are to be divided. Yet because of all the street advice that fills the heads of my prospective clients, I spend a significant amount of time dispelling myths that have been fed to them.

Since the legal process tends to move slowly, my role in each of my client's lives on a day-to-day basis during the divorce case is rather limited, and I am wholly absent from their lives once the divorce is finalized. However, the acquaintances who feed my clients nonsense and thereby create emotional angst have daily access, sometimes with calamitous consequences.

⸻

One of the tools I have to employ with a client who has unrealistic expectations about the divorce process is discussing the cost of litigation—meaning the legal expenses they will have to pay to me to take their case from start to finish—as a means of opening their eyes as to what it will set them back to have the knock-down, drag-out fight they desire. This is where a hype man in your life can do you a disservice. It is not their money, after all, so they have no problem telling you how to spend it.

Along with saying "water is wet" and "the sky is blue," there is no more obvious statement than "most lawyers are happy to take your money." Not all lawyers will counsel you to save your money by forgoing a fight about the principle of something. In all my years of practicing divorce law, I have had only a handful of cases where, at the time of the final hearing, my client and their soon-to-be ex-spouse were still fighting over the household belongings. At a billable rate of $300 per hour or more, it makes no sense for most people to fight over their used furniture, appliances, cookware, utensils, linens, and electronics. For the cost of a few billable hours, most people's household items can be replaced with used counterparts on Craigslist or Facebook Marketplace. All of the stuff at issue is used. Thus, it makes no sense for my clients to pay me to "fight" for things that are not economically worth it.

Yet some people have the hankering to battle their soon-to-be-ex in court, just for the sake of fighting. They take the position that "giving in" is not an option because they do not want the other person to "win." I use "win" in quotations because quite often, the only winners in these types of cases are the attorneys who each receive thousands of dollars in fees from their clients whose motivation is to cause their former partner financial and emotional pain.

You will have no difficulty finding representation if you take the position that you want to engage in scorched-earth litigation with your soon-to-be ex-spouse over the principle of something—and you have the money to pay for it. Though, if you want to divorce your spouse because he is a lying egomaniac, and you have no money, assets, children, or debts to fight about, there is no reason to pay an attorney a lot of money to divide nothing. If your spouse cheated on you and you want revenge, the divorce court is not going to issue a ruling that admonishes your spouse for breaking your marital vows and decreeing them to be a "horrible person." That is simply not what the court does.

I bring this up because there are people in your life who will rile you up to the point that you can find yourself paying thousands of dollars for a fight that will yield you nothing in return. Here is a common example of how this happens:

Tina tells her best friend, Karen, that she is filing for divorce and that because there is not much to fight over other than a 2012 Honda Accord, some furniture, and retirement funds, it should be a quick and painless divorce. Tina is upset that her husband, Ike, cheated on her, and she is angry that Ike is entitled to half of her retirement that she saved during the marriage because he blew all of his money at the casino every week of their marriage. Of course, Karen agrees with Tina. Karen, a non-attorney but well-meaning confidant, tells Tina that Ike is a "jerk," "should not get a dime" from her, and that she should "fight Ike for every penny." Karen tells Tina about her hairdresser's sister who "got everything" in her divorce "because the husband cheated," and Tina's outcome should be no different.

Sure enough, Tina hires an attorney and gives her the instruction "to fight tooth and nail" instead of trying to resolve the case amicably through a dissolution as the attorney originally suggested. Despite the attorney advising Tina that a dissolution would require a $1,500 retainer versus the $4,000 for a divorce, Tina— still riled up from her best friend's pep talk—demands that a divorce action be filed right away. The attorney complies with her client's request. At their next meeting, Karen congratulates Tina on her decision.

Over many happy hours in the weeks and months that follow, Tina tells Karen that Ike "wanted a quick divorce" because there was nothing to divide. Karen repeatedly echoes Tina's initial response that she would be giving Ike exactly what he wants if she makes the process easy on him. Instead of giving him what he wants, Tina wants Ike to feel pain, just like he caused her.

Following her client's instructions, Tina's attorney issues subpoenas, takes Ike's deposition, files a myriad of motions, and diligently works the case as her client instructed so Ike would have to pay his attorney to counteract the onslaught. Despite being informed by her attorney about the cost of litigating in this manner, as well as being given best-case, worst-case, and likely scenarios for taking the case to a final hearing, Tina demands the fight persist.

Three months into the litigation, with the $4,000 initial retainer depleted and another $1,500 still owed to the lawyer, Tina starts to panic. She gets a call from her attorney demanding payment on her bill, plus an additional $2,000 to replenish her retainer. The lawyer informs Tina that the cost of getting through the final hearing would likely be another $3,000 to $5,000 out of pocket. Tina calls Karen, who again repeats her talking points that to give in now would be to give Ike exactly what he wants. Karen tells her friend, "Don't let him win!" before hanging up the phone.

Now, months into the litigation, Tina is left to decide whether she is going to try to resolve the case—as she should have done months ago—or if she is going to press forward while her legal expenses continue to mount when she will likely get nothing from taking the matter to a contested final hearing.

Every week, I talk with a prospective client who has been hyped up for a fight that they either cannot afford or would be fruitless for them due to the expense. If you have someone in your life who riles you up the way that Karen riled Tina up, they are the wrong person to talk to about your problems, especially when your finances are involved.

There are times when a battle in the courts is necessary, and there are times when it makes no financial or legal sense to do so. Any reputable attorney should be able to identify whether the fight you want to have is worth the expense. The overwhelming majority of divorce cases are resolved without the need for a contested final hearing because the law tends to be clear and the result is predictable. In some cases, however, especially when children are involved, knock-down-drag-out litigation is the only course. But that is not every case. If you get fired up to have a legal fight because you have a friend constantly talking in your ear instigating you to do so, you will likely find yourself in an expensive and protracted battle that will leave you with a drained bank account and yield nothing of substance from the court.

Someone in a short-term marriage with no children, no assets, and nothing to divide should not incur thousands of dollars in legal fees to terminate their marriage. Likewise, I regularly get calls from prospective clients who want to file motions to terminate their ex-spouse's parenting time because of a minor scratch to their child's body that occurred on just one occasion, but have no other evidence of abuse. I meet with people who want to pay me to try to reduce their child support arrearage, even though they have no legal basis to do so and would be better served by paying the money they were going to pay me toward their arrearage. The list goes on and on.

I have countless conversations with clients and prospective clients who want to protract their cases, drive up their legal expenses, and try to cause their former partner financial and emotional pain—all while emptying their bank accounts in the process. That, to me, is the absolute worst use of their money.

Early in my practice, I became involved in a never-ending case that I inherited from a retired attorney where the parties had been back to court six times in the eight years since they had divorced. At my first court appearance on the case at the scheduled pretrial conference, the judge, who was all-too-familiar with the parties and their litigious history, called everyone into the courtroom, looked at the parties' financial affidavits, and asked each whether they had set aside anything for their children's college. Neither had saved a dime.

The judge then said to the parties, "*Well, you can pay for your own kids' college, or you can pay for the tuition of your attorneys' kids, because that's what you're doing right now—your choice. I would suggest that the two of you sit down, start acting like adults, and stop spending all of your money on attorneys that you cannot afford to have fights over things that the two of you need to work out on your own.*" While gruff in his delivery, the judge stated the obvious: the ex-spouses were spending their children's college fund fighting each other. Thankfully, for their children's sake, that was the message they needed to hear. They resolved the matter on their own shortly thereafter.

Despite my frugal and pragmatic guidance, I still have clients who prefer to break open the checkbook because they want a fight for the sake of a fight. Others heed my advice and appreciate the resolution to their legal problem in an expeditious, cost-effective manner. The fundamental difference between these two types of clients is that the ones who ignore my advice and look to pick a fight are often heavily influenced by friends, family members, and coworkers who hype them up in such a way that my guidance is drowned out by a chorus of instigators who stoke their emotions.

You have people in your life who somehow fire you up in a way that others do not. That visceral response is helpful in some situations, but not in others. Take time to consider and recognize the difference between the people in your life who fire you up in a good way versus those who do it in a negative way. The bad influencers certainly exist, and their methods can be subtle. I doubt anyone close to you wants to see you harmed, but the net result of advice may nudge you towards the wrong path because they stoke your emotions, which then cloud your judgment.

This is a long way of saying that not all advice you receive is good advice. Avoid conversing about your divorce and personal finances with hype men, enablers, and the broke people in your life because their input, whether solicited or unsolicited, can only set you back on your financial journey.

MISTAKE #7:
NO GOALS. NO PLAN.

One of my more memorable former clients, Toby, was so emotionally wrecked by his divorce that he lacked confidence in seemingly every aspect of his life. He had a bachelor's degree but was working a low-paying, second-shift factory job in a booming economy. Toby struggled with the prospect of rejection from prospective employers, so he stayed put in a position well below his qualifications. Each rejection seemed to pour salt into Toby's open wounds, which was understandable considering that he was still in love with his ex-wife and was having a difficult time coping with the divorce that she initiated.

Yet, Toby's unwillingness to put himself out there and find a better job not only hurt his finances but also his ability to spend time with his kids. Since Toby was working from 3 p.m. until 11 p.m. Monday through Friday, he was unable to have any time with his children after school during the week. Moreover, his job required him to work mandatory overtime on some Saturdays, which further impeded his ability to spend time with them on his weekends. Between the low pay (relative to his education) and the limited amount of time he had with his kids due to his work hours, nothing about Toby's employment was positive. In addition to confidence, Toby lacked any sort of plan to bring about change to his life.

> *Everyone has a plan until they get punched in the mouth.*
>
> **– Mike Tyson**

Toby's entire world was rocked by his divorce and understandably so. He had a broken heart and seemed to have lost everything he loved. Even worse, he was stuck in a dead-end job and lacked hope. The life he was living was not the one he had envisioned, and it was obvious that whatever plans he once had unfortunately evaporated the moment he was served with divorce papers. I could tell that, deep down, Toby knew he needed to make changes, and those changes would greatly improve his life. I wanted him to make those changes in a way that was right for his future. He simply was not ready.

After Toby's divorce was finalized, I made it a point to keep in touch with him. I wanted to be a voice of encouragement for him and genuinely wanted to see his situation improve. He was a kind man with a good work ethic. It made no sense to me why he could not get a better job with typical first-shift hours, and one that utilized his college degree. If Toby landed a better paying job with better hours, he would be able to spend significantly more time with his children. Certainly, I figured, the prospect of making more money and spending more time with his children would motivate him to act.

I started emailing Toby links to various job websites and local companies that had vacancies. I set up direct lines of communication for Toby to speak to business owners I knew who were always looking for qualified people. Nevertheless, Toby never followed through on any lead, and eventually he stopped responding. The last I heard, he was still working the same dead-end job with the same restrictive hours and presumably at the same wage. Nothing had changed. As much as I wanted better things for Toby, and as much as I wanted to create a plan for him, he did not want it for himself—at least not on the same timeline that I wanted it for him.

It would be disingenuous for anyone to dictate the amount of time one should need before they can be expected to recover, emotionally and financially, from any life-changing event as impactful as a divorce. I made that mistake with Toby and regret nudging him when he was not ready. It certainly is a delicate balance, especially when someone is in a rut.

> *Only I can change my life.*
> *No one else can do it for me.*
> **– Carol Burnett**

We all know people like Toby. We want something better for them. We all have someone in our lives who we wish would quit smoking or drinking, lose weight for the sake of their overall health, move on from a bad relationship, or get their act together. The harsh reality is that what we want for someone other than ourselves cannot be accomplished without that person wanting it for themselves. While we may be able to provide support, encouragement, and inspiration, we cannot make someone change who has no desire to change.

Toby's situation reminds me of an iconic scene from one of my favorite Christmas movies, and universally recognized as one of the greatest movies of all time, Frank Capra's *It's a Wonderful Life*. I always seem to tune into the movie when it is on TV halfway through, so I rarely catch the opening scene. The movie begins on Christmas Eve. As the camera pans the streets and buildings of fictional Bedford Falls, New York, the audience hears voices of various loved ones of protagonist George Bailey, who are all praying for him in his time of extreme need:

GOWER'S VOICE: I owe everything to George Bailey. Help him, dear Father.

MARTINI'S VOICE: Joseph, Jesus, and Mary. Help my friend, Mr. Bailey.

MRS. BAILEY'S VOICE: Help my son George tonight.

BERT'S VOICE: He never thinks about himself, God; that's why he's in trouble.

ERNIE'S VOICE: George is a good guy. Give him a break, God.

MARY'S VOICE: I love him, dear Lord. Watch over him tonight.

JANIE'S VOICE: Please, God. Something's the matter with Daddy.

ZUZU'S VOICE: Please bring Daddy back.[21]

As the audience quickly learns, George has given up hope. At the time, he does not know that people all around town are praying for him and asking for help from above. By the end of the film, George realizes the true extent of his family and friends' love and support, and his faith and hope are restored. Despite the countless memorable parts of the movie, it is always the opening scene that resonates with me the most when I encounter someone who has lost hope, like my former client, Toby.

I know that you have hope. You are reading this book because you want to take steps to improve your life. That gives me hope, and whether you realize it or not, it should give you hope too. You want tomorrow to be better than today, and you

---

21. IT'S A WONDERFUL LIFE (1947).

are proactively taking steps to do something about it. Be proud of that.

Just as George Bailey had lots of people praying for him during his time of need, right now there are people in your life who are rooting for you. They are well aware of the rocky road you have traveled and want you to be able to recover in all aspects of your life—emotionally, physically, spiritually, and financially. Yet, as much as they want success and happiness for you, *you* are the one in control.

You are the catalyst for any change in your life. If you take the right steps in the right direction, then your support network will feel more empowered to offer encouragement and tools in their arsenal to aid you in your journey. We all want to help someone who wants to help themself. Yet, the first step must be taken by you. Only you can make the changes to your budget, spending, career, and plan. It does not matter how much time you have been treading water or how you got here. It does not matter if your divorce was finalized ten weeks or ten years ago; you are reading this now because you want to make a change in your life. As part of your recovery process, and as discussed in Part II of this book, your next steps will to write down your goals and then plan out a course of action to achieve them.

> *A dream written down with a date becomes a goal.*
> *A goal broken down into steps becomes a plan.*
> *A plan backed by action makes your dreams come true.*
>
> **– Greg S. Reid**

One of the biggest mistakes I see divorcees make is having no plan or goals. Regardless of whether your goals are physical, emotional, or financial, writing them down is of utmost importance. So too is setting a date. If you talk to your friends about your dream of "one day" running a marathon, that dream is vastly different than saying, "*I am going to run a marathon within the next six months.*" I have a colleague who says that he stops listening when his friends and coworkers start a sentence with: "*I have been thinking about getting into* _____ [fill in the blank hobby]." Why? There is a big difference between "thinking of getting into" something and taking steps to get into it.

Writing down your dream and putting parameters on it makes it a goal. If your goal is to lose weight, how much weight? And in what amount of time? If my goal, for instance, is to lose 15 pounds by my birthday, I have an actual target to hit on the scale and a date by which I intend to hit that target. I must lose five pounds first. However long it takes me to lose five pounds will help me figure out the amount of time I will need to lose ten, then 15 for my target to be realistic. This timeline and definitive mark allow me to break my goal down into attainable steps.

So, if you want to run a marathon in six months, you need to devise and follow a plan to build your endurance so you can ultimately run 26.2 miles. Marathon runners typically follow a schedule with daily and weekly mileage goals based on a timeline that leads up to the day of the marathon. If you stick to a plan like that, you will be physically conditioned and ready to finish the marathon on race day. Crossing the finish line of any journey of this magnitude is an accomplishment and a testament to the level of discipline, pain, and sacrifice you can endure, as is losing the weight you set out to cut or saving a certain amount of money that you set out to save.

Your career, finances, and all other life areas where you wish to achieve any significant goal require the same goal setting, planning, discipline, and execution. You will not attain success in any major aspect of your life without planning.

So, what are your goals? What areas of your life do you want to improve? What is the timeframe in which you can accomplish these goals?

> *Discipline is the bridge between goals and accomplishment.*
>
> **– Jim Rohn**

If you are like most people, you desire to achieve greater success in your career beyond where you are at now. For many, though, deciding how to accomplish this can be overwhelming and difficult to figure out. Fortunately, I can recommend a good place to start: the podcast and writings of Ken Coleman. Ken Coleman's podcast, called *The Ken Coleman Show*, is a fantastic tool if you feel lost when it comes to deciding on your career path or are unsure what steps to take to improve your prospects. Ken takes calls from people and provides them with guidance on how to get out of a rut, ask for a raise, or determine the next chapter in their working life.

Ken's website, *KenColeman.com*, has various resources that you may find valuable, such as his free "How to Win the Interview" and "How to Write the Perfect Resumé" articles to assist you in landing your dream job. Ken also gives much-needed guidance on how to ask for a raise in your current position, the best way to position yourself for a promotion, and things you can do to increase the opportunities in your field.[22]

22. I would be remiss if I failed to point out that no amount of budgeting and belt-tightening can solve a situation where your income is so low that it is all paid out just to cover basic life expenses. Most personal finance authors—and much of this book—overlook that cold, hard truth. If this describes your situation, you desperately need a raise or a job change. I understand that something as simple as a flat tire could bust your budget for the month and put your job in jeopardy. That makes the status quo of staying in such a low-paying job unsustainable. I don't have easy answers for you other than the basic encouragement to keep looking and applying for better employment, and continue trying to hone your skills so

Practically speaking, without knowing where you want to end up, it is hard to map out a plan on how to get there. Having no idea where you want to land career-wise is no different than walking into a travel agency and telling the travel agent you want to go somewhere but have no idea where. You must decide on the destination first.

Maybe your goal is to start your own business. If this is the case, I can recommend several places to start. Christy Wright's book *Business Boutique: A Woman's Guide for Making Money Doing What She Loves*, and the *BusinessBoutique.com* website are dedicated to helping women take an idea and turn it into a thriving business.

Dave Ramsey's book *EntreLeadership: 20 Years of Practical Business Wisdom from the Trenches*, the EntreLeadership podcast, *EntreLeadership.com* website, YouTube videos, and EntreLeadership live events are all dedicated to the same mission—helping you build your business and take it to new heights.

Merely saying "I want to make more money," without a plan or knowing the type of position where you want to eventually land is the daydream mindset you must break. Making more money requires a higher performance at your current job, a promotion in your chosen career field, or even a new endeavor altogether. If switching employers or even changing your career will allow you to achieve your greater financial goals, now is the time to start taking steps to make your dreams come true. What

---

you can be of great value to your employer and in your industry. You may have to move to a different city in a different state or enter an entirely new industry. If a change of venue is necessary for you to improve your future, do it for yourself and your family tree. Mike Rowe (most famously known from his television show *Dirty Jobs*) has published some of the most insightful and motivational content out there on trades and work. Visit his website at *MikeRoweWorks.org* for more information, and search YouTube for his keynote speeches if you truly want to be inspired.

is it that you want to do with the next chapter of your life? Where is it that you want to go? Where do you want to be ten years from now? What about 20 years? Or 30 years?

> *If you aim at nothing, you will hit it every time.*
>
> **– Zig Ziglar**

After the haze of your divorce wears off, it is up to you to answer these questions. If the storm clouds are still overhead and you have difficulty thinking about next week, let alone ten years from now, I assure you that the storm will pass. When it does, it is time to decide your precise goals so you can formulate the plan you will need to follow to achieve them. The longer you delay setting and working towards your goals, the longer you can expect things to stay the same as they are right now.

To help inspire my clients, I frequently have discussions with them about the future. My hope in initiating these discussions is to jump-start their long-term planning during a time when they are focused on the immediate future and help them realize that the areas of disagreement they had with their ex-spouse are no longer holding them back.

Did your ex-spouse hate to travel? Was your ex so bad with money that you could never afford that dream vacation? Nothing is standing in your way of saving money for your dream vacation. That trip to see the Colosseum in Rome, the Sistine Chapel in Vatican City, and the Eiffel Tower in Paris can be in your future if you save money for it. The same holds for the cruise your ex-spouse never wanted to take or that trip to the beach your ex said was too far away.

Did your ex-spouse stifle your career ambitions? Well, that naysayer is no longer a roadblock. If you want to go back to school, nobody is stopping you. You do not have to ask for permission or have a fight about it with anyone. You only have one mind to convince that your plan is a good one, and you are in total control of it.

Setting goals in all aspects of your life—big and small, personal and professional—will give you something to work toward so you do not spend the next years of your life treading water and going nowhere. The more defined the goals are, the better you'll understand what you need to do to accomplish them.

Part II of this book will assist you in developing a plan to get out of debt, build an emergency fund, save for retirement, set aside money for your children's higher education, pay off your house, and build wealth so you can be generous and live your best life. Ultimately, the plan will lead you to financial independence. It is time-tested, and it has helped millions before you; it will help you too if you follow the steps with precision and discipline.

Before we dive into the particulars of the plan, I want to stress the importance of starting your financial recovery *today*. Explaining and showing you the mathematical cost of waiting is my best and closing argument as to why you cannot afford any further delay.

Compound interest is the game-changer you'll miss out on if you don't get started right away.

Compound interest occurs when the money you have invested gets reinvested so you earn interest on the interest. If you invest $1,000 and earn 10% interest on that money annually, at the end of one year you will have $1,100 (the $1,000 you invested plus $100 in interest).

The following year, your interest is not just $100 because your investment is now $1,100. Therefore, assuming your 10% return, you have $1,210 (the $1,100 you invested plus $110 in interest) after two years. In the third year, a 10% return on your $1,210 investment yields you an account balance of $1,331 ($1,210 + $121 in interest).

Earning interest on your already-earned interest, over time, is what allows you to build wealth. Therefore, every year you do *not* invest is a lost opportunity to harness the power of compound interest.

> *Compound interest is the eighth wonder of the world.*
>
> *He who understands it, earns it.*
> *He who doesn't, pays it.*
>
> **– Albert Einstein**

Let's look at the impact of saving $850 per month, which is what many people collectively spend every month on their car payments, restaurants, and cable subscription. The chart below shows you that you can reach $1 million—thanks to compound interest—by investing $850 every month (or $10,200 annually), at 8% interest, for 28 years:

Year	Starting Balance	Annual Contribution	Growth (Interest Earned)	Balance at the End of the Year
1	$0	$10,200	$816	$11,016
2	$11,016	$10,200	$1,697	$22,913
3	$22,913	$10,200	$2,649	$35,762
4	$35,762	$10,200	$3,677	$49,639
5	$49,639	$10,200	$4,787	$64,626
6	$64,626	$10,200	$5,986	$80,813
7	$80,813	$10,200	$7,281	$98,294
8	$98,294	$10,200	$8,679	$117,173
9	$117,173	$10,200	$10,190	$137,563
10	$137,563	$10,200	$11,821	$159,584
11	$159,584	$10,200	$13,583	$183,367
12	$183,367	$10,200	$15,485	$209,052
13	$209,052	$10,200	$17,540	$236,792
14	$236,792	$10,200	$19,759	$266,752
15	$266,752	$10,200	$22,156	$299,108
16	$299,108	$10,200	$24,745	$334,052
17	$334,052	$10,200	$27,540	$371,792
18	$371,792	$10,200	$30,559	$412,552
19	$412,552	$10,200	$33,820	$456,572
20	$456,572	$10,200	$37,342	$504,114
21	$504,114	$10,200	$41,145	$555,459
22	$555,459	$10,200	$45,253	$610,912
23	$610,912	$10,200	$49,689	$670,801
24	$670,801	$10,200	$54,480	$735,481
25	$735,481	$10,200	$59,654	$805,335
26	$805,335	$10,200	$65,243	$880,778
27	$880,778	$10,200	$71,278	$962,256
28	$962,256	$10,200	$77,796	$1,050,253
	Total:	**$285,600**	**$764,653**	**$1,050,253**

By year ten, the interest earned exceeds $11,000 per year—which is more than the annual contribution. By year 20, the accumulated total is over $500,000, and the annual interest earned is more than $37,000 per year. By year 28, the interest earned is more than $75,000 per year, and the total value of the account exceeds $1 million.

If you put $850 in a cookie jar every month for 28 years and get a zero percent return (or, more accurately, a negative rate of return due to inflation), you will have $285,600. As you see in the table above, the overwhelming majority of what you earn— in this case, $764,000, which is nearly triple what you invested— is interest on the interest of what you invested every year for 28 years. This is how compound interest works incredibly well in your favor. If we were to expand this table out over an even longer timeframe, the results are staggering. After 35 years, the total grows to $1.89 million. At 40 years, the total is $2.85 million.

The key component to compound interest is TIME.

If you only have a short amount of time to invest, your deposits will not have enough time to accrue interest on the interest. As shown by the compound interest calculation above, if you invest $850 per month for ten years, the result is not anywhere close to that achieved with a longer amount of time for interest to compound.

Moreover, when you have a short timeframe to invest, most of what you will have in your account must come from your deposits, not the interest you have earned because the money has not had the time to achieve interest on the interest from the earlier years. By comparison, to reach $1,000,000 in ten years, at the same return of 8% annually, an investment of $5,500 every month (or $66,000 annually) is necessary.

Year	Starting Balance	Annual Contribution	Growth (Interest Earned)	Balance at the End of the Year
1	$0	$66,000	$5,280	$71,280
2	$71,280	$66,000	$10,982	$148,262
3	$148,262	$66,000	$17,141	$231,403
4	$231,403	$66,000	$23,792	$321,196
5	$321,196	$66,000	$30,976	$418,171
6	$418,171	$66,000	$38,734	$522,905
7	$522,905	$66,000	$47,112	$636,017
8	$636,017	$66,000	$56,161	$758,179
9	$758,179	$66,000	$65,934	$890,113
10	$890,113	$66,000	$76,489	$1,032,602
	Total:	**$660,000**	**$372,602**	**$1,032,602**

The bottom row of the table shows that two-thirds of the account balance comes from the sum of the deposits (totaling $660,000)—not the interest (totaling $372,602)—because there has not been enough time for the deposits to accrue substantial interest. It is undoubtedly much easier to save $850 a month than saving $5,500 a month. As such, the longer your timeframe, the easier it will be for you to achieve great wealth with consistent, modest investment amounts over several decades. Time is the x-factor.

If your goal is to build wealth, you can only capitalize on the glorious benefits of compound interest if you have a longer period in which to invest your money. This is why it is vital to start *today*.

Any further delays will have lifelong consequences for you. The two tables show you, in black and white, the impact of investing the same amount of money over a short period versus a long period, with wildly differing results due to the awesome power of compounding interest.

I hope that after reading Part I, you have a clear understanding of all the ways your financial progress can be potentially hindered as you walk this journey. If you continue to maintain the lifestyle post-divorce as you did during your marriage, you will never get ahead. If too much of your money is going toward housing, you won't have enough money at the end of every month to pay down debt or invest. If you continuously engage in retail therapy instead of coming up with a budget and sticking to it, your bank account will always be empty. And if you allow your ex-spouse, your internal Melodramatic Alter Ego, and the financially-unsavvy hype men in your life to manipulate you and your finances, you can expect your financial recovery to drag on forever.

So, set goals and establish a plan so you can move forward meaningfully. You will be able to progress steadily toward financial success now that you're aware of all the common money mistakes that occur after divorce. Now let's get to work on your plan.

Part II:
Your Post-Divorce Financial Recovery Plan

Divorce has set you back by stripping you of both time and money. Since time is a key component of building wealth, burning more daylight is not an option. You cannot risk wasting years following the wrong "expert" or drifting aimlessly without a plan. Now that you know the mistakes to avoid, we must address the all-important question: *where do I go from here?*

On the one hand, the answer is simple—you need a plan. On the other hand, doing everything necessary to follow that plan is where the real challenge lies. This section of the book is devoted to helping you formulate your next steps and develop your plan to achieve a full financial recovery from your divorce.

Your path will depend entirely on your starting point or, put even more simply, on whether you have debt. If you have any debt besides your mortgage, the first stage of your journey will focus on eliminating it. Once you have eliminated all of the debts except for your mortgage, your focus will be building up your emergency fund, investing for retirement, and paying down your mortgage at an accelerated rate while continuing to live debt free. When your house is paid off, you are able to invest significant amounts of money every month, maximize your retirement contributions, and supercharge your ascent to achieving financial independence. We have to walk before we can run, which means each stage is attacked individually instead of trying to do everything at once. By the end of Part II, you will know exactly what you need to do next, what resources you will need to follow to guide you through to the next stage, and will be armed with the tools to help you along the way.

———————◉———————

Rules of the Road: Foundational Financial Principles For All

Despite your starting point and academic knowledge of personal finance, four basic foundational principles apply to anyone walking the journey towards achieving financial success.

1. You must be committed to becoming debt-free and remaining debt-free.

If you are in debt, a portion of every paycheck you receive is already earmarked to leave your bank account before you have a chance to do anything else to make that money work for you. Think of how much money you could save and invest every month if you did not have to pay the mortgage, a car payment, loans for repairs you financed, medical debt, student loans, or credit card bills. Yet by having any or all of the aforementioned debts, which siphon off your monthly income, you restrict your ability to save and invest.

Therefore, if you have debt, you must be committed to getting out of it, which calls for a one-two punch: (1) eliminate the debt you have, and (2) pledge never to take on any new debt. While it may seem like a radical move to pay cash for everything you purchase from here on out—including your next car, vacation, appliance, and home renovation—this is exactly the mentality you will develop and what you will be able to do if you follow the plan outlined in the coming pages.

2. *A few bad financial decisions can cause you to regress quite quickly.*

A significant portion of Part I of this book is dedicated to educating you on all the ways you can rapidly and easily go from being financially sound to saddled with debt. Consider the damage you can do in just one day. Within the next 24 hours, you are fully capable of financing a high-priced sports car, booking a luxurious vacation on credit, and buying a brand-new furniture set, wardrobe, and home theater, all on new store-issued credit cards that the checkout clerks will happily offer to you.

Dave Ramsey frequently says that debt is the most aggressively marketed product in our society. He is 100% right. If you do not believe that is the case, carry around a pen for the next two days and put a mark on your hand every time you see any sort of advertisement for debt. At the end of every car commercial, you will see terms for financing and leasing. That is an advertisement for debt.

The next time you are at the grocery store, pay attention to the advertisements on the bottom or back of your receipt or plastered all over the checkout station for the store's credit card. You are being pitched debt for the sake of saving $0.10/gallon on your gas. When you're at a retailer and propositioned with an offer for their credit card, you're being pitched debt. Capital One, Visa, American Express, and Mastercard—companies that make money by charging people late fees and 28% APR interest—seem to have unlimited budgets for television commercials, direct mail, and print advertisements. In fact, for every unsolicited credit card offer that hits your mailbox, your email inbox filters out two times as many. Every HVAC, plumbing, home repair, and window company will offer you financing terms, as will every home furnishing and mattress retailer. "*Ninety days same as cash*" and "*0% financing for 12 months*" are introductory teaser periods that try to trick you into thinking that the debt you are voluntarily taking on is not actually debt. Nevertheless, these are indeed all forms of debt that are promoted and marketed in such a way as to try and convince us otherwise.

Therefore, although you may be in a good financial spot right now, there are powerful and creative vendors continually trying to lure you either back into debt or deeper into debt. As such, your commitment to taking on no more debt—and adhering to that commitment—becomes even more vital so you don't find yourself making payments for years because of regrettable decisions made on a bad day.

3. *You must have your own "why."*

Your *why* is your reason—or, more likely, a bunch of reasons—for wanting to make a change, take control, and depart from the path you have been traveling up until now. Say your answers out loud to the following questions, and then write them down:

> *Why do I want to get out of debt?*

> *What was "the straw that broke the camel's back" that led me to want to make a change?*

> *What are my financial goals?*

> *Where do I want to be financially in five years? Ten years? 20 years?*

> *What do I want my lifestyle in retirement to look like?*

> *What are the things I wish I could do if I were financially stable?*

Let's be clear: these are all very complicated questions. You may find it challenging to put your answers into words. Instead of struggling with the existential, consider the following responsive statements that are shared by many who are in the same boat as you:

- *I'm sick of working 40 to 60 hours a week and having nothing to show for it.*

- *I'm tired of being broke.*

- *I'm tired of living paycheck to paycheck.*

- *I'm sick and tired of being sick and tired.*

- *I hate the anxiety I feel every time I open the mailbox and see statements from all of the places where I owe money.*

- *I want to retire eventually, but I don't have nearly enough saved.*

- *I don't know if I'll ever be able to retire.*

- *Money fights led to problems in my prior marriage, and I do not want money to cause me problems again in future relationships.*

- *I need to get rid of these student loan payments.*

- *After I pay my bills, I have no money left to save, invest, enjoy, or give.*

- *I don't even know how much debt I have.*

- *If I had a $500 emergency, I could not pay for it without borrowing money.*

- *I want to help my kids pay for college so they don't end up deep in student loan debt.*

- *I'm scared.*

- *I don't know what I'm doing with my money.*

- *I don't know how to invest.*

- *I don't want to be a burden on my family when I'm older and unable to work.*

Do any of these resonate with you? A few certainly resonate with me. All of us wonder and worry about retirement, investing, and the impact that a job loss or medical incident would have on our lives. There is no shame in being scared. There is no dishonor in acknowledging feelings of anxiety around your finances, future, and ability to handle this next chapter of your life. There is no indignity in seeking guidance to help you figure out a plan, just like you are doing by reading this book.

Getting out of debt to free up money to save for emergencies and your future might be your *why*. Paying off your car so you have an additional $500 every month to set aside for your child's college fund might be your *why*. Saving for retirement so you can travel the world and not be the 85-year-old still having to work might be your *why*. Being able to sleep soundly at night without worrying about money might be your *why*. Your *why* might be all of the above.

> *More important than the **how** we achieve financial freedom is the **why**. Find your reasons **why** you want to be free and wealthy.*
>
> **– Robert Kiyosaki**

Identifying what has lit a fire under you to come this far is essential to the process. You are the person who will have to put in the hard work to achieve your goals. These *whys* should help you identify your goals and motivate you when you encounter setbacks along the way. They are the reasons why you're making these sacrifices and why you need to press forward.

So, write your goals and *whys* down. Do it now. Put them on an index card and stick it in your wallet or purse. Take a picture of it with your cell phone. This way, when you experience a moment of frustration, hopelessness, or discouragement, you can pull out this list to remind yourself why you are making these changes in your life.

4. You must be intentional with your money—meaning you must be on a budget.

The word budget appears in this book more than 150 times. Why? Because your success in getting out of debt, staying out of debt, and winning with money is entirely dependent upon your ability to formulate a monthly budget and stick to it. Whether you make $2,000 a month or $20,000 a month, you will have nothing to show for it if your expenditures exceed your income.

Budgeting 101

Budgeting is the act of assigning every dollar of your monthly income a designated role. Creating a budget is relatively simple to do. I have broken it down into several steps to illustrate each one's importance and the basic methodology.

First Step: List all of your monthly income. To start, write down your total take-home income from all sources (job income, child support, spousal support, pension, bonus, overtime, gratuities, income from other jobs, etc.) for the upcoming month. Note that not every month's income will be the same, as sometimes you might sell something, receive overtime or a windfall, get an extra paycheck or tax refund, or even find forgotten cash in your coat pocket.

> *A budget is telling your money where to go instead of wondering where it went.*
>
> **– John Maxwell**

Second Step: List all of your monthly expenses. Housing (rent/mortgage payment), insurance, utilities, groceries, debt payment minimums, transportation, personal care items, clothing, entertainment, subscriptions, memberships, internet, and cell phone expenses are all line items that tend to be on almost everyone's budget. Add whatever other line item expenses you have for this specific month. You may also have irregular, one-time expenses, such as a car repair, or expenses that are billed quarterly or annually, that also need to be included in your budget for the upcoming month.

Third Step: Subtract your monthly expenses from your monthly income. Whatever amount is left over can be applied to your debt. If you do not have enough income to cover your expenses, you need to adjust your budget allocations. You are not in congress, so you cannot run a deficit every month.

Fourth Step: Create a "zero-based" budget by accounting for every dollar of your monthly income. Consider the following illustration of Allison's budget for July:

July Income

Paycheck #1	$1,850
Paycheck #2	$1,850
Child Support	$1,100
Babysitting	$200
Total Income:	**$5,000**

July Expenses

Rent	-$1,050
Groceries	-$650
Utilities & Internet	-$160
Insurance (Auto & Renters)	-$100
Minimum Debt Payments*	-$1,200
Cell Phone	-$50
Netflix & Gym Membership	-$50
Child's Clothing	-$50
Child's Haircut	-$20
Entertainment	-$100
Auto - Fuel & Oil Change	-$70
Total Expenses:	**-$3,500**

As you will see in the table above, Allison has minimum debt payments of $1,200 per month. In total, she has $17,400 in debt as of July, which is broken down as follows:

Creditor Name	Outstanding Balance	Minimum Monthly Payment
Capital One Credit Card	$ 600	$100
Dr. Thomas, DDS	$ 800	$100
Lowe's Credit Card	$1,200	$200
Valley Hospital	$5,300	$400
Toyota Finance	$9,500	$400
Total:	**$17,400**	**$1,200**

For this to be a zero-based budget—which means that every dollar is accounted for and nothing is left over—the remaining $1,500 of Allison's income (which is found by subtracting her monthly expenses of $3,500 from her monthly income of $5,000) must be assigned a role. So, if she adds a line item of $1,500 for extra payments toward her outstanding debts, every dollar of her income in July will have a particular purpose. In other words, there is intentionally nothing left over at the end of the month because every dollar has been used on its specific assignment.

Fifth step: Rinse and repeat. Create a budget every month and readjust it as needed. Doing a budget has never been easier, thanks to the advent of apps and websites devoted to assisting people in creating and staying on budget. Two of the best are YNAB.com (which stands for You Need A Budget) and EveryDollar.com (which is named after the idea of giving every dollar an assignment each month). YNAB has a nominal monthly fee, while EveryDollar has both free and premium versions available. If you don't find either of these interfaces user-friendly, check out Mint.com, which has a popular, free budget feature that is used by millions. If using an app will make budgeting easier for you, thereby making it more likely that you'll follow your plan, use the app. If you prefer using Excel or writing everything out on a pad of paper, go for it. Just be sure to do your budget every month and follow it. In other words, do what works for you.

The most difficult months are the first few when you are trying to figure out if your allocations for things like groceries and utilities are sufficient. Like anything else, the more experienced you become, the quicker and easier the process will be. Your budget may initially take you 60 to 90 minutes to put together; later, it might only take six to nine minutes because you can look at prior months, see where you over- and under-allocated, and adjust appropriately.

If you are paid biweekly, two months every year you will get three paychecks instead of two. These extra paycheck months are a prime opportunity for you to allocate most, if not all, of the extra money you receive toward your immediate goals. You will know those months well in advance, so you will be able to plan accordingly as you get a better grip on your finances.

Sixth step: If you are having trouble sticking to your budget, use the envelope system. Those who are single may find it challenging to have no accountability partner. If you overspent when you were previously married, your partner would have likely said something to you about it, perhaps even challenged your expenditure. Then again, that feedback may be one of the reasons you got divorced. Nevertheless, now there's a good chance no one puts forth any opinions about your spending because you can easily keep your finances a secret from even your closest friends and family members. So, if you find yourself struggling to follow your budget, there are two things I suggest: (1) trying the envelope system and (2) finding an accountability partner.

The envelope system has been around for generations and was commonly used by our grandparents and great-grandparents long before credit cards and our "cashless" society came into existence. It is quite simple to implement: for each category of expenditures in your budget, take out the allocated amount in cash and put it in an envelope. For instance, if your monthly budget allots $150 for restaurants, write "Restaurants" on an envelope and take $150 out of the ATM or bank in cash on the first day of the month. Then, for the rest of the month, only spend the cash that is in the envelope when you go to a restaurant. If you want to go to one dinner and spend the entire $150, that is certainly your prerogative. Conversely, if you want to dine out ten times for $15 each, you can do so because you have the money in your envelope to spend that month. Just be sure to pay cash for that specific category using only cash from that envelope. If the money runs out before the last day of the month, you have no more to spend on restaurants and cannot go out to eat.

With the envelope system, the envelope is your immediate accountability partner; if it's empty, you're cut off until the next month rolls around. This is an effective way to ensure that you do not cheat on yourself and your budget by overspending. Additionally, using actual bills and coins—meaning you will physically watch the currency disappear as you hand it over to the clerk when you pay for things—will serve as a more tangible reminder that you are spending your budgeted money than simply swiping a debit card.

Whenever students in a *Financial Peace University* seminar I am coordinating (or individuals who I'm coaching one-on-one) tell me that they are having difficulty staying on track with their budget, I tell them to start small and use the envelope system. Groceries, restaurants, and entertainment are the three categories that most people overspend when they start budgeting.

Budgeting for groceries can be particularly tricky because it is a mixture of *wants* and *needs*. There is a difference between needing food to eat and wanting the organic, grass-fed, Wagyu ribeye steak with a side of crab legs. Groceries are also a significant monthly expense, as anyone with growing children knows all too well. Therefore, it is quite common for those new to budgeting to struggle with their grocery allocation. Much like restaurants, it is an area where people frequently do not realize how much they spend every month until they start tracking their expenditures.

Be sure to give yourself grace the first few months you try to stay on a budget. You will likely under-allocate some categories, over-allocate others, and forget some expenses altogether. This is normal and part of the learning curve. Do not give up. Once you have three or four months of budgets under your belt, you will have a strong sense of your actual monthly expenses in every category, and you will then be in a position to recognize the areas where you can cut back your spending to pay down debt or aggressively save.

If you prefer one-on-one help, ask a friend, coworker, or family member who is good with money to assist you with budgeting. Whenever a coworker or friend has asked me for advice on a financial topic, I have always taken the time to help. Honestly, I think this is the ultimate compliment, and I imagine many others feel the same way. Although personal finance is not often openly discussed among friends or coworkers, those who have their financial affairs in order are almost always happy to share their knowledge with someone who speaks up and asks for guidance.

A common excuse people use for living without a budget is that they do not want to be told how to spend their money because a budget deprives them of the freedom to spend in whatever manner they please, whenever they please. This is the absolute wrong way to look at budgeting. Your budget is not your enemy. It is not your mother, father, or even your ex-spouse telling you what to do or not do with your money. You are in control of the budget, which means you are the one for giving out the assignments to each dollar of your income for that month.

Your budget gives you freedom. When you have allocated your money to a specific expense, you have the freedom to spend that predetermined amount for that particular expenditure that month without any guilt. If you allot $150 per month on entertainment and you attend a concert that costs $125 for your ticket and $25 in food and beverages, you have done nothing wrong! You are simply spending the money you allocated for this very reason, which means that you should enjoy the show and feel no guilt. The problem arises when you have assigned $150 to entertainment for the month and you spend $500. Or worse, you're sitting on thousands of dollars of debt but regularly spend $500 per month on entertainment while racking up 28% interest on your credit card balances.

If restaurants are that important to you, then budget money for restaurants. The same principle applies to any daily vices, clothes, small and large luxuries, or just about any *want* in your life. You are in charge of your budget, which means that you can spend your money on all of the above so long as you stick to your budgeted amounts and ensure you have money left over to apply to your goals. If you consistently blow your budget and ignore the monthly spending parameters you have set for yourself, you will have breached the agreement with yourself. It is no different than setting out to lose weight by sticking to a diet, only to ignore it and hit the pizza buffet with regularity.

In addition to freedom, your budget gives you predictability. Considering Allison's July budget, for instance, she can predict the precise timeframe of her debt payoff so long as she continues to stick to the budget and apply any extra money directly toward funding her goal, which is to become debt-free. If she can pay $1,500 extra per month toward her debt—on top of the $1,200 she has already accounted for in the line item "Minimum Debt Payments"—she will be able to pay off her debts in seven months versus the 15 months it will take if she pays nothing but the minimum payments (of $1,200 per month, even after her smaller debts are extinguished.)

Also, if Allison has an unexpected repair bill come up in any given month, she can build it into her budget during her quest to pay off her debts, she can immediately change her game plan by paying only the minimum on her debts that month, and spend whatever is leftover on the repair or life events she will encounter instead of filling out a credit application or accumulating additional debt. This audible may add a month to her journey, but that is life—not everything goes perfectly according to plan. The most important part is that she will be able to adapt to the unexpected situation and avoid taking on more debt.

Budgeting allows Allison to identify the temporary cuts she is willing to endure to speed up her debt payoff. In Allison's July budget, she has cut out restaurants, left herself and her son a small amount for entertainment, and is forgoing a summer vacation because her focus is on paying off her debt as fast as possible. She has maximized her ability to squeeze every dollar possible from her income and supercharged her ability to get this debt gone from her life. Next July, she will be in a position to take that summer trip with her son; the difference is that next year's trip will be paid for using cash instead of using borrowed funds.

Of course, the alternative to living on a budget is to have no plan whatsoever for your money. This may sound familiar to you. If you have made no progress doing it your way without a budget, you simply cannot expect things to change and is thus all the more reason to get on a budget starting today.

Keep in mind that budgeting is a lifelong endeavor and isn't just for those in debt. It is a necessary monthly requirement for anyone who wants to build and maintain wealth. Someone who is debt-free and sitting on several million dollars in investments *still* must stay on a budget or risk going broke. Their budget may include larger, more lavish expenditures, but overspending will drain any stockpile of savings if it exceeds the monthly income. There are plenty of broke ex-pro athletes and former A-list celebrities who have unfortunately proven time and again that one cannot sustain a lifestyle where the expenditures exceed the income.

Therefore, regardless of your starting point, the key to your success will depend on your resolute adherence to a monthly budget.

There are many ways up the mountain to reach the summit of financial freedom. My goal here is to show you the best path.

Imagine what it would be like to be financially free. You would be free to quit a toxic job, travel wherever and whenever you want. You can read a restaurant menu from left (meal options) to right (prices) instead of looking at the prices first and making a choice based off what is inexpensive. You would be free from the shackles of debt, and any anxiety whatsoever about money because you'll have saved to take care of yourself and your family for the rest of your life.

> *Working because you want to, not because you have to, is financial freedom.*
>
> **– Tony Robbins**

Financial freedom means different things to different people. And your version of freedom might be achieved with a $500,000 net worth, while your best friend's version might require $5 million. But regardless of the amount it takes for you to reach your goal, our destination is essentially the same—our own personalized vision of financial freedom. There are many paths up the mountain. You can win the lottery or inherit the money from a long-lost distant relative. Or, you can trek up to the top of the mountain on your own by following an intentional plan.

I have devoted the rest of this section of the book to showing you the best path that you can personally take to reach your version of financial freedom.

In writing this book, I chose not to reinvent the wheel or devise a brand-new financial plan for you as a divorcee. Fantastic time-tested debt-elimination and wealth-building methods already exist. They have been crafted and honed by others who have dedicated their lives to helping people get out of debt, save for retirement, and build wealth. Their plans are not necessarily tailored to divorcees; if they were, I would not have written this book. Nevertheless, now that you are armed with the information from Part I, you are well-positioned to follow the writings and teachings of three of the most brilliant individuals I have encountered in my study of personal finance: Dave Ramsey, John "Jack" Bogle, and J.L. Collins.

For a brief moment, I toyed with the idea of developing a one-size-fits-all, comprehensive plan of my own to include in this book. But that thought only lasted a moment. It was a fleeting idea because I have long known that no one can create a better get-out-of-debt plan than Dave Ramsey, an author and radio show host who has helped millions of people pay off their debts. Similarly, I cannot write a better book on investing than Jack Bogle, the founder of The Vanguard Group and "father of index fund investing" who has helped tens of millions of people maximize their investment returns through indexing and minimize the fees that eat away at those returns. Finally, financial expert and author J.L. Collins' book called *The Simple Path to Wealth: Your Roadmap to Financial Independence and a Rich, Free Life* not only offers fantastic guidance but is simple and direct enough that anyone can follow it—regardless of whether you are new to the world of personal finance or are very educated on the topic—as it maps out the journey to the ultimate goal of achieving financial independence.

While there is an endless supply of books, podcasts, and articles trying to tell you how to win with money, these three authors are the absolute best of the best. Sure, this will involve more reading, more of your time, and continued attention. But we are talking about your financial recovery, which absolutely needs to be a priority for you because of the setback you have endured.

If it is more important to you to spend your time finding out who received the rose, got voted off the island, and won the big game than you do on furthering your personal finance education, that is certainly within your rights. However, if you want to be successful in eliminating debt, rebuilding the percentage of your net worth that was lost in your divorce, and saving for your retirement, you'll need to spend more time and energy on your financial education beyond this book. Taking control of your finances is no different than getting in shape; you can't go to the gym once and expect to be in the best shape of your life. You must devote regular and purposeful time and energy to your mission, and your technique can make a world of difference.

Before we get into the specifics, I want you to know that I receive absolutely no compensation for recommending any authors, publications, websites, or tools in this book. Any outside author I endorse has been chosen based on my own experiences in not only consuming their digital content and reading their books, blog posts, and articles, but also in personally adopting their teachings. Even with my zest for knowledge on the subject of personal finance and investing over the past two decades, I made an untold number of dumb financial mistakes, tried to do things my way, and long ago was the equivalent of a ship at sea without a compass or plan.

At various times along my journey, I followed the advice of self-proclaimed "experts" who I thought were knowledgeable. I wasted too much time doing the wrong things and listening to the wrong people. My purpose here is to direct you to the experts who I know will assist you in achieving your immediate and long-term financial goals because their teachings have worked for me. Your divorce has stripped you of time and the option of burning daylight. Following the wrong plan—or operating with no plan at all—will set you back more than you can afford. So, let's get moving.

The Plan Details

Your starting point on this journey is determined by the level of debt in your life. Identify the stage that most closely resembles your current situation:

STAGE ONE: The Debt Elimination Stage. You have non-mortgage debts, including but not limited to credit card debt, student loans, car loans, medical debt, personal loans, a home equity loan, etc. (individually, as a co-signor, or as a guarantor.)

STAGE TWO: The Mortgage Elimination & Nest Egg Growth Stage. You have no consumer debt, but you have mortgage debt or are saving to buy a home.

STAGE THREE: The Wealth Accumulation & Preservation Stage. You have no debts whatsoever, and you own your residence outright.

If you are in Stages Two or Three, please do not skip the Stage One discussion. Unfortunately, you might quite easily find yourself in debt one day, by choice or happenstance; if you go from having no debt to having it again, you'll need to know how to get it cleaned up as fast as possible.[23]

---

23. Similarly, if you are in Stage Three, read the Stage Two section because it is instructive for your situation as well.

STAGE ONE:

The Debt Elimination Stage

If you have debt of any kind, follow Dave Ramsey.

Do you have car loans, student loans, medical bills, personal loans, credit cards, lines of credit, an outstanding debt owed to your family or friend, legal debt, or any type of installment plan? If you answered *yes* to any of these, you're in Stage One and your journey starts here.

The plan you should follow is taught by Dave Ramsey. He is a financial counselor, nationally syndicated radio talk show host, and best-selling author who has taught millions of people how to get out of debt over the last 25 years. His radio talk show, aptly titled *The Dave Ramsey Show*, is carried on hundreds of radio stations daily and available to you for free as a podcast. He has authored several books, including *The Total Money Makeover: A Proven Plan for Financial Fitness*. He also teaches his methodologies through live events and via a nine-week program known as *Financial Peace University* that can be accessed online and attended in-person at a church or community center in your area.

Ramsey teaches a program called the "Baby Steps," which builds off of a program that was taught by the late Larry Burkett of Crown Financial Ministries. Given the outreach of both Ramsey and Burkett, it is likely that someone you know follows their teachings. Both employ a seven-step methodology that focuses on eliminating debt before saving and investing:

	Dave Ramsey's Baby Steps[24]	Larry Burkett's Money Map[25]
Step 1	Save an initial $1,000 for your emergency fund.	Save an initial $1,000 for your emergency fund.
Step 2	Pay off all debt using the Debt Snowball method.	Pay off all credit cards and increase your emergency fund to one month of living expenses.
Step 3	Save up an emergency fund of three to six months of expenses.	Pay off all consumer debt and increase your emergency fund to three months of living expenses.
Step 4*	Invest 15% of your income into retirement plans.	Begin saving for retirement, major purchases (home, car, etc.), and children's education.
Step 5*	Save for your child(ren)'s college education.	Buy an affordable home, pay off your home mortgage early, and keep investing for retirement.
Step 6*	Pay off your home mortgage early.	Your home mortgage is paid off and children's education is funded; ensure your estate plan is in order.
Step 7	Continue to build wealth and generously give to others.	Retirement is funded so you can be generous with your time and money.

*Steps 4 to 6 of the Baby Steps are to be done simultaneously.

I am an advocate for the "Baby Steps" plan because you will assuredly see results if you follow it. Also, and more importantly,

---

24. *The Total Money Makeover: A Proven Plan for Financial Fitness* is the book that outlines Dave Ramsey's Baby Steps. Borrow it from your local library or buy it on Amazon. It is foundational reading, and it should be the very next book you read after you finish this book.

25. *The Crown Money Map*, Crown Financial Ministries, https://www.crown.org/wp-content/uploads/2017/11/Crown-Money-Map.pdf (last visited 10/4/2020).

Ramsey and his team are constantly generating digital content to answer nearly every conceivable personal finance question that you might have in your journey to become debt-free. If you search Google using the phrase in quotes "Dave Ramsey" plus your question, I am 99.9% certain that Ramsey has at least one article on his website, a clip from his radio show, and a YouTube video where he provides an in-depth explanation succinctly and straightforwardly to address your query. This way, you will quickly find answers to the follow-up questions that will assuredly arise as you travel your journey. I am, without reservation, fully confident that the content published by Ramsey and his team will answer most anything you could ask. Moreover, the answers will be delivered instantaneously and at no cost to you. The man provides a life-changing service to his millions of followers.

You do not have to spend a dime to learn the get-out-of-debt lessons taught by Dave Ramsey. You can simply borrow his books from your local library, watch his videos on YouTube, read the articles on his website, and listen to his daily radio show/podcast—all free of charge. He is not peddling a get-rich-quick program; in fact, he often says that he is in the "slow cooker business," not the "microwave business," because there are no shortcuts when it comes to getting out of debt and building wealth.

If you are in any sort of non-mortgage debt, Ramsey is the sherpa who will take you up Stage One of the mountain.

⸺●⸺

Start by reading Dave Ramsey's book, *The Total Money Makeover*.

The Total Money Makeover is necessary follow-up reading because it spells out the Baby Steps in complete detail. If you're in debt, your initial and immediate focus is on a one-two punch of saving up $1,000 as a beginner emergency fund, followed by eliminating your debts from smallest to largest using a technique called the Debt Snowball.

Compile a list of all your debts and put them in order from smallest to largest.

Take out a pen and pad of paper or open a spreadsheet on your computer. Start by listing all of your outstanding debts from smallest to largest, and include the following information about them:

Creditor Name	Outstanding Balance	Minimum Monthly Payment
	Grand Total:	**Total Monthly Minimum Owed:**

For some, compiling this list will be a daunting task. You may have old, stale debt that is in collections. If you have avoided this task previously because you simply did not want to know the size of the hole you are in, fear not—this is a necessary part of the journey. Knowledge is power. From this list, you will learn the amount it will take for you to become debt-free, and you will identify your monthly minimum debt obligations for your budget.

If you have lost track of old debts, obtain a copy of your credit report for free by going to *AnnualCreditReport.com*. Be careful, though. If you simply search Google for "free credit report," websites will pop up that try to charge you for something that should be free. On your credit report, you will see outstanding debts in your name, and whether any creditor or collections agency has reported debt as outstanding or delinquent to the three credit bureaus.

While your credit report is a good place to start when compiling your list of outstanding debts, it is not necessarily comprehensive. For a debt to appear on your credit report, it must have been reported by a creditor or debt collector. Medical, consumer, and legal debts are not always reported. Similarly, personal loans owed to family and friends will not appear on your credit report, nor will recent debts you owe to medical care providers or utility companies. So, you may have to proactively contact past medical providers, for example, to see if you have an outstanding balance. If you are current on your debts to entities like hospitals, doctor's offices, utilities and your divorce lawyer, they will probably not appear on your credit report because the only time those types of debts tend to appear is when they are reported by a debt collection agency as being delinquent and in collections.

As discussed in Part I, Mistake #4 (Not Knowing and Enforcing the Terms of Your Divorce Decree), it is your responsibility to pay attention to what is required of both you and your ex-spouse in your divorce decree when it comes to your debts. You may be responsible for paying a debt in the name of your ex-spouse or vice versa. Your ex-spouse's court-ordered responsibility to extinguish debt in your name will not be reflected on your credit report. Consequently, you need to monitor your ex-spouse's payments and compliance with the court order. Also, if you are legally responsible for a debt in the name of your ex-spouse, be sure to include it on your list.

Use the Debt Snowball (vs. Debt Avalanche) to pay off your debts.

When it comes to paying off debt, there are two primary methodologies. The first is called the "Debt Snowball," and it involves paying off your debts in order from smallest to largest (with the exception of your mortgage, which will be covered in Stage Two), regardless of the interest rate. When following this method, you make minimum payments on all your debts, and you throw whatever money you have leftover in your budget at the smallest debt until it is extinguished. Then you take the money that was previously used to pay the minimum payment of your smallest debt and apply that to the next debt on the list. At this point, the snowball starts to gain in size and momentum. Once you are down to your fourth debt on the list, for example, you have the minimum payments you were paying on the three smallest debts—which you have successfully eliminated—to add to the fourth debt's minimum payment, plus whatever money you can squeeze out of your budget.

The alternative method is the "Debt Avalanche," whereby you list your debts in order of interest rate and pay off the debts with the highest interest rates first. If you have credit card debt with a 28% interest rate, a student loan with a 7% interest rate, and a 0% HVAC replacement loan, by following the Debt Avalanche method, you will pay off the credit card first, then the student loan, and then finally the HVAC debt.

Both the Debt Snowball and Debt Avalanche are well-proven methods that take you to the same destination: being debt-free. Yet, there are advantages and disadvantages to each and, therefore, advocates and opponents of each.

The Debt Snowball is the method that is taught in the Baby Steps plan. I, too, recommend this methodology because it is what I used to become debt-free, and it is what I have seen many people use to achieve great financial success. I believe the Debt Snowball is the most effective way to get rid of your debt because it gives a psychological boost by showing you quick results due to your changed behavior.[26]

Eliminating debt is often compared to losing weight. If you start a diet and workout regimen but don't see any results despite several weeks or months of meticulously sticking to the program, you'll probably end up quitting it. But suppose you lose a couple of pounds after two weeks and five pounds after the program's first month. In that case, you will become a believer in its effectiveness and are more likely to continue adhering to it because it has already proven effective. The Debt Snowball follows the same logic. With its focus on eliminating your smallest debts first, the Debt Snowball will show you early results, much like the effective weight loss plan, which should motivate you to stick with it.

Conversely, the Debt Avalanche is aimed at saving you money. Proponents of the Debt Avalanche would say that every dollar you throw at a loan with a 0% interest rate instead of the credit card debt is being wasted because you will continue to accrue interest on the credit card by carrying a higher balance for a longer period of time. Therefore, your motivation should come from all of the interest you are saving by paying off your debts with the highest interest rates first, not from quick victories of eliminating smaller debts.

---

26. A free and helpful tool worth mentioning is Undebt.it, which can be found by visiting *www.undebt.it* (it's a secure site, just registered with a .it suffix instead of .com because of the play-on-words). Undebt.it allows you to visualize and track your progress, project your payoff date, and show you the impact of various scenarios of increasing your income and applying one-time payments from selling things, bonuses, and windfalls.

To help you visualize the difference between the two methodologies, let's look at Todd's use of the Debt Snowball to eliminate his debts totaling $60,000.

Creditor Name	Outstanding Balance	Minimum Monthly Payment
Home Depot credit card	$500	$ 75
Pella Doors credit card	$900	$100
Dr. Adams	$1,400	$200
Student Loan #1	$2,700	$200
Student Loan #2	$8,000	$250
Honda Finance	$22,500	$550
Student Loan #3	$24,000	$400
Total:	**$60,000**	**$1,775**

In addition to his minimum payment obligation totaling $1,775 per month, Todd can squeeze $1,225 out of his budget, which allows him to pay $3,000 per month toward his debt. Using the Debt Snowball method, Todd will make the minimum payments on all of his debts and use the additional $1,225 to pay off the smallest debt first. Then, using the earmarked funds squeezed out of the budget, Todd extinguishes the $425 balance of the Home Depot credit card (remember, he already paid a $75 minimum monthly payment) and uses the remaining funds to pay off the $800 balance on the Pella Doors Credit Card (after the minimum $100 was paid). So, in one month, Todd eliminates two of his debts—the Home Depot credit card and Pella Doors credit card (a total of $1,400) and frees up the $175 of minimum monthly payments from those two debts to now throw at the next debt on his list.

For the second month, Todd's remaining debts are as follows:

Creditor Name	Outstanding Balance	Minimum Monthly Payment
Home Depot credit card	$0	$75
Pella Doors credit card	$0	$100
Dr. Adams	$1,200	$200 + $75 + 100 = $375
Student Loan #1	$2,500	$200
Student Loan #2	$7,750	$250
Honda Finance	$21,950	$550
Student Loan #3	$23,600	$400
Total:	**$57,000**	**$1,775**

Todd pays off the third debt on his list (Dr. Adams) by making the $375 minimum payment and using $825 out of the $1,225 earmarked from his budget; the remaining amount he applies to Student Loan #1. In just two months, Todd has eliminated three debts and freed up $375 per month to be put on the minimum payment of the next debt on his list.

For the third month, Todd's remaining debts are as follows:

Creditor Name	Outstanding Balance	Minimum Monthly Payment
Home Depot credit card	$0	$75
Pella Doors credit card	$0	$100
Dr. Adams	$0	$200
Student Loan #1	$1,900	$200 + $200 + $75 + 100 = $575
Student Loan #2	$7,500	$250
Honda Finance	$21,400	$550
Student Loan #3	$23,200	$400
Total:	**$54,000**	**$1,775**

Todd makes the minimum payment on Student Loan #1, applies the minimum payment amounts from the eliminated debts, and the entire $1,225 squeezed from his budget (collectively totaling $1,800), leaving him with a balance of only $100.

Todd continues onward with this process. By the end of the fourth month, Todd's outstanding debts are as follows:

Creditor Name	Outstanding Balance	Minimum Monthly Payment
~~Home Depot credit card~~	~~$ 0~~	~~$ 75~~
~~Pella Doors credit card~~	~~$ 0~~	~~$100~~
~~Dr. Adams~~	~~$ 0~~	~~$200~~
~~Student Loan #1~~	~~$ 0~~	~~$200~~
Student Loan #2	$5,300	$250 + 200 + 200 + 100 + 75 = $825
Honda Finance	$20,300	$550
Student Loan #3	$22,400	$400
Total:	**$48,000**	**$1,775**

At this point, Todd is on a roll. He sees the fruits of his labor and is quite motivated to keep up his progress. He has wiped out four debts, freed up $825 per month, and knows that the Debt Snowball method is working for him. With $48,000 to go, Todd will be done with his Debt Snowball in roughly 16-17 months if he can continue to pay $3,000 per month toward his debt.

Of course, Todd may consider the amount of time left and think that it is too long. In the divorce settlement, he agreed to keep the Honda Pilot SUV and its accompanying debt with Honda Finance because he knew his ex-wife could not afford it. Todd soon realizes that if he can sell the Honda Pilot SUV for what he owes and instead purchase an older but reliable used car, the duration of his journey will be cut down significantly because he will instantly eliminate $20,300 in debt and free up an additional $550 per month.

One of the advantages of the Debt Snowball method is that Todd can hit pause at any time. If needed, he can pay the required minimum payments and choose to use the minimum payment money from the eliminated debts to tackle any immediate financial issues or needs that arise.

Continuing with this example, in the fifth month, Todd decides to sell the SUV and use the $1,225 he normally earmarks for debt, the $550 from his former car payment, and the $575 from the four debts he has already eliminated to purchase a used Honda Accord for $2,350. Now, with no car payment, going into the sixth month, Todd's remaining journey is as follows:

Creditor Name	Outstanding Balance	Minimum Monthly Payment
~~Home Depot Credit Card~~	~~$0~~	~~$75~~
~~Pella Doors Credit Card~~	~~$0~~	~~$100~~
~~Dr. Adams~~	~~$0~~	~~$200~~
~~Student Loan #1~~	~~$0~~	~~$200~~
Student Loan #2	$5,050	$250 + 200 + 200 + 100 + 75 + 550 = $1,375
~~Honda Finance~~	~~$0~~	~~$550~~
Student Loan #3	$22,000	$400
Total:	**$27,050**	**$1,775**

By selling the SUV, Todd is able to eliminate all the remaining debts in his name in roughly nine months. Todd's early and sustained results demonstrate the value and effectiveness of following the Debt Snowball method.

Notice that Todd's debt payoff strategy pays no attention to interest rates. The Debt Snowball system dismisses the concept of interest rates as a motivator because saving money on interest is not nearly as important as persevering and continuing with the program until the end.

Let's now consider what Todd's debt-elimination strategy would look like by using the Debt Avalanche.

Creditor Name	Outstanding Balance	Interest Rate
Home Depot credit card	$500	28.99%
Pella Doors credit card	$900	0%
Dr. Adams	$1,400	1.5%
Student Loan #1	$2,700	4.9%
Student Loan #2	$8,000	5.9%
Honda Finance	$22,500	0.99%
Student Loan #3	$24,000	6.3%
Total:	**$60,000**	**$1,775**

Following the Debt Avalanche, Todd's strategy would be to pay off the Home Depot credit card (at 28.99% interest) first, followed by Student Loan #3 (at 6.3% interest), and so on. With the same $1,225 amount earmarked towards debt, Todd would see the Home Depot credit card extinguished in the first month but would not have any other victories for quite a while. With its heavy emphasis on interest rates, the Debt Avalanche would keep Todd's low and no-interest loans around until the end of his journey, thereby depriving him of the early and frequent victories he experienced while using the Debt Snowball method.

The argument in favor of the Debt Avalanche is that it is mathematically advantageous to pay off the highest interest rate first, thereby saving you money in the long run. However, Todd was not using math when he got himself into $60,000 of debt; his behavior reflected his mindset that debt was an acceptable way to pay for the things he did not have the cash to cover. He needs to totally change both his mindset and behavior to get out and stay out of debt. If he takes steps to get out of debt but does not view it as the enemy, he is going to find himself back in the finance office at the car dealership and agreeing to open up a Target credit card the next time it's offered to him.

Your situation is no different. The Debt Snowball method will show you results if you stick with it, squeeze every dollar possible out of your budget and throw it at your debt, and maintain your intensity over the months or years it takes to become debt-free. It will also aid in the transformation of your financial mindset, which will be of great value to you over the rest of your life.

———————————●○———————————

Maintaining focus is essential to getting out of debt.

Getting out of debt is hard work. It is obviously way easier to go into debt than it is to get out of it. You can fill out a credit application and buy a new car in a couple of hours while paying that car off will take you years of your life. Plus, you have already been through the wringer emotionally, physically, and financially as a divorcee. Thus far, every page of this book has been devoted to showing you how to home in on your financial goals while simultaneously teaching you to ignore the internal and external voices that say it is okay to spend because doing so will temporarily make you feel better.

Achieving any substantial goal in life—becoming debt-free, losing a lot of weight, or climbing Mt. Kilimanjaro—takes a level of grit many people do not possess. You have survived everything life has thrown at you so far. I know you have it in you to dig deeper and get yourself out of debt. Depending on the size of your debt, the victories may not come for months or even years. Moreover, depending on the kind of lifestyle you lived during your marriage and post-divorce, gaining traction in this journey might require making radical changes in your life.

This is why staying motivated is of the utmost importance. Here are my tips for staying energized and focused on what could possibly be a multi-year journey toward freedom from debt.

1. Use a visual aid to help track your progress.

Back when you were in preschool, your class probably worked on a project where you strung together strips of construction paper in a chain so you could count down to a special day by tearing one ring off the chain every day. This was a good way for you as a child to visualize how many days you had to go until the end of the school year. Despite the decades that have passed, this type of tool is still effective.

Find a visual aid that you can use to track your progress as you pay down your debt. I am a fan of putting marbles, each of which represents a certain dollar figure of debt, in a vase; every time you make a payment, take out the appropriate amount of marbles to represent the amount of debt you just eliminated. Put the vase in your kitchen or on your bathroom countertop so you see it every day. Many people use a paper thermometer that they color in for each chunk of debt eliminated.

Whatever visual aid you decide to use, make sure it is something you don't mind having around for a while and in a location in your home where you will see it daily. Make the units of measurement small enough that you can mark your progress every month or so. The aid is a subtle reminder of the amount of work ahead to achieve your goal and of the progress you have made to date.

2. Celebrate the small victories and milestones.

If you have never before been able to save up a $1,000 emergency fund or pay off $2,500 in debt, then doing so is a reason to celebrate. Paying off your car is cause enough to pop a bottle of champagne, as is eliminating your student loan debt. For larger debts, pick $5,000 or $10,000 milestones along the way to commemorate.

Whichever way you decide to celebrate your accomplishments and milestones, just make sure the cost doesn't derail your progress. If you have committed to avoiding restaurants to get debt-free, reaching a major milestone is worthy of a reasonably priced restaurant visit. Whether your reward is going to a concert or even taking a weekend getaway, milestones are the perfect opportunity to pause for a minute and reflect on your tremendous achievements.

If you face a particularly long debt-free journey, plan a substantial reward for yourself in recognition of reaching the summit. If you have $60,000 in debt and you know that it is going to take you two or three years to pay it off, it is helpful to have something to look forward to in order to keep you motivated, such as a trip to be taken only after you reach your goal. Paying cash for that trip to Italy to celebrate becoming debt-free will be an accomplishment you will remember for the rest of your life.

3. Use personal finance podcasts, books, and digital content to help you maintain focus.

If you like to browse Facebook and Instagram during your free time, you are voluntarily subjecting yourself to images of people experiencing lavish activities and self-proclaimed "influencers" whose "job" it is to push you to buy material things. People post pictures of vacations, gourmet meals, concerts, and themselves out and about—that is, things that cost money. No one posts pictures of themselves sitting at home watching reruns of *The Office* for the fifth time.

It can be detrimental to your mindset to regularly expose yourself to images of people you may or may not personally know on a beach in some exotic locale, posing in front of the stage at some weekend concert festival on the other side of the country, standing next to the new car they just bought, or eating out at a fancy restaurant for the third time this week. Yet, in moments of world-weariness, this is what we voluntarily do to ourselves.

I have found that one way to counteract the malaise of social media is to use your free time to improve yourself by listening to personal finance podcasts (such as *The Dave Ramsey Show*) and audiobooks that reinforce your mission. John C. Maxwell, Jim Rohn, Zig Ziglar, Tony Robbins, and Meg Meeker are all terrific authors whose books will motivate you as you wash dishes, work out at the gym, do your laundry, and on your commute to work. They are all well-known and popular enough that you should have no difficulty finding them on audiobooks and in print at your local library.

Even outside of social media, we are inundated with advertisements aimed at separating us from our money. A podcast or audiobook that preaches personal responsibility with money is the antithesis to every advertisement because it underscores your mission to save money instead of spending it, pay down debt instead of incurring it, and ignore the temptation to buy things you don't need instead of succumbing to it.

4. Attend Financial Peace University or a live or online event.

I am a concert fanatic. I enjoy seeing my favorite artists play live because the memories of the experience stay with me for months and years afterward. It is hard to walk out of a concert featuring your favorite band and not feel energized. The good news is that there are also live programs that will inspire you to remain enthusiastic and energized throughout your entire financial recovery.

Starting in 2016, I began leading *Financial Peace University* ("FPU") classes, Dave Ramsey's nine-week personal finance curriculum, out of my law firm's conference room. FPU covers the Baby Steps plan and includes lessons on paying off debt, saving for retirement, purchasing and paying off your home, insurance, and your generosity once you are completely debt-free. FPU is offered in-person and online, but I suggest the in-person option if one is available in your area.

Each of the nine classes starts with a video lesson, followed by a small group discussion. In this environment, you will find class coordinators who donate their time and energy to help you and your classmates win with money. More importantly, you'll also discover a group of accountability partners who can share in your initial successes and struggles. After years of leading this class, I still think it is worth my time because of all the people I can help; I certainly think it is worth yours as well because it can help you get energized, stay motivated, and become even more educated on important topics in personal finance. You will also see that you are not alone in your journey since you will be surrounded by others in your community dealing with the same issues as you.

In addition to FPU, Ramsey and his team conduct many live and virtual events. If a $20 ticket to one of these events boosts your motivation for a few months, it is worth every penny.

5. *Find a like-minded friend (or two) who is walking the same journey and can be your accountability partner, sounding board, and sympathetic ear.*

If you are doing this alone right now, I strongly suggest trying to find someone who is willing to accompany you on this journey as your accountability partner. Having a close relationship with someone who allows you to talk candidly about your finances can make a significant difference. We all have bad days. We are all susceptible to an impulse buy, engaging in retail therapy, and destroying this month's budget. Having a trusted confidant who you can call when you need a respected voice to remind you to maintain your focus is no different than the trainer in the boxer's corner pumping him up and telling him to keep fighting because he can win the bout in the 12th round.

There are a handful of people in my life who I can, fortunately, be open and honest with about my finances, including my struggles, setbacks, and goals. When I am about to make a big purchase, it is nice to have friends who will help me reflect on the terms and necessity of the purchase before moving forward. Whenever I am frustrated by a setback—such as a major home or automobile repair—I am able to vent my frustrations to friends who are kind enough to remind me that things in life don't always go according to plan. I serve the same role for them too and act as a sounding board when they have questions and difficulties in their own journeys toward financial independence.

When looking for an accountability partner, the number one quality is them having their financial act together. This does not necessarily mean someone must be debt-free or independently wealthy to be a good accountability partner. Far from it. Someone with $100,000 in student loan debt can be a fantastic accountability partner if they know how to budget, are aggressively and successfully paying down their debt every month, and are vocal enough to challenge you and educate you on ways you can tighten your budget. Someone who tries to comfort you by saying "*you deserve nice things*" and "*don't worry about having a car payment or student loans because everybody has debt*" is the exact opposite of what you need in an accountability partner.

Furthermore, your accountability partner does not need to be a close friend or even someone you know very well. Your best friend, who you have known since preschool, might be terrible with money. Rather, your reserved and frugal coworker who knows everything about saving and budgeting could be a tremendous help to you in your journey. There is no shame in asking someone you believe to be good with money if they can help you with your budget. Your confidant may end up being a thrifty family member or a volunteer financial counselor from your church. Frugal people *love* to share tips about how to be frugal. I know this because I'm one of them.

6. Shave months off your debt-free journey by selling things, picking up extra work, and making temporary sacrifices.

Part I advocates extricating unaffordable things from your life. It is up to you to follow through and actually make the change. If your car value is dropping like a rock and the monthly payments are slowing your ability to pay off other debts, sell it. If your house payment is making you house-poor, make a change. Don't hesitate to sell things you no longer can afford, need, or want. Once you have wiped out your debt and no longer have to worry about monthly debt payments, you can quickly save up cash to purchase the car, toys, and things you sacrificed to get out of debt.

Until then, it is worth making sacrifices you may have never made before just to shorten your timeframe of getting out of debt. Limiting the amount you dine out, forgoing vacations, not upgrading to the newest cell phone, replacing your expensive car with a cheaper one, picking up extra work, and scouring your budget every month to see where you can save an extra $50 per month are all signs of someone who is acting with an admirable intensity and a commitment to getting out of debt as fast as humanly possible.

Getting rid of debt requires a complete change in mindset and behavior. In a society where debt is normalized, being the person with none will make you abnormal. You will need to view debt as your enemy and as something that you will never accept in your life again once you've finally escaped it. Making short term sacrifices for the sake of becoming debt-free will set you up tremendously well for long term success.

7. *Give yourself grace.*

You are going to make mistakes along the way. There will assuredly be setbacks. In any given month, you may discover that you have an old tax debt that was previously unknown to you. A car repair, medical incident, or set of new tires might cost you hundreds of dollars you had planned to throw at your debt. These unexpected life events will inevitably happen. My advice here is to give yourself grace. Nothing is going to go 100% according to your plan, even if you do everything right. However, just like riding a bike, if you fall, brush yourself off, and get back on. Avoid the temptation to get angry at yourself and the world because dwelling on the things that went wrong can derail all your progress. One day, so long as you stick to the plan, an unexpected $1,500 car repair will merely be a nuisance and not a reason for tears and an emotional breakdown.

8. *Follow the plan.*

Seriously, the best advice I can give you—and anyone in debt who wants to get out of debt—is to read *The Total Money Makeover* and to follow the Baby Steps exactly as they are presented. I cannot rehash everything covered in the book, nor would I want to; it is polished, time-tested, and a proven method for you to eliminate your debt. In addition, *The Total Money*

Makeover will teach you so much more, including your next steps of saving up a full 3-6-month emergency fund, saving for retirement, paying off your mortgage early once you all of your other debts, and the importance of giving as part of your journey to financial freedom.

If you follow the Baby Steps, I do not doubt that that you will be able to tackle your debts with a vengeance. As soon as you are done with this book, start reading *The Total Money Makeover* and follow the plan exactly as prescribed. When you cross the finish line of paying off all of your debts, you will join millions of people who followed the same steps to become debt-free and are ready to start Stage Two.

***

STAGE TWO:

THE MORTGAGE ELIMINATION & NEST EGG GROWTH STAGE

Once you are out of your consumer, medical, automobile, personal, and student loan debt, your next step is to save up an emergency fund large enough to cover three to six months of your expenses. Since you do not have any monthly payments or debt obligations beyond your mortgage, you are in a position to save quickly, focus on investing for your retirement and your children's college, and pay extra on your mortgage so you can reach the point of being completely debt-free.[27] In other words, this is the time for you to build wealth and grow your nest egg.

---

27. If you are renting and therefore do not have a mortgage, still read this section (even though you are in Stage Three). Every extra dollar you can squeeze from your budget to set aside for a down payment will result in a lower mortgage, that is if you eventually decide to purchase a home.

Just as I recommended to those in Stage One, your starting point in Stage Two is to read *The Total Money Makeover*. According to the Baby Steps as laid out in the book, once you have your fully-funded emergency fund, you are in Baby Steps #4, #5, and #6, which are intended to be done simultaneously. Each month, Ramsey recommends investing 15% of your gross income into your retirement account (Baby Step #4), setting aside money for your child(ren)'s college fund (Baby Step #5), and then using the rest of the money left over in your budget to pay down your home mortgage early (Baby Step #6)—in that order of priority. *The Total Money Makeover* explains the methodology for these simultaneous steps in a crystal-clear manner, as well as the logic behind the plan. So, your next move after you finish this book is to keep reading.

It is my sincere hope that this book, along with *The Total Money Makeover*, inspires you to dive much deeper into the world of personal finance and investing. After all, when you're debt-free, you have money to save and invest. If you want that money to grow, you need to know where to put it. The problem, though, is that when you know nothing about investing, you are susceptible to making poor investment decisions, following the wrong guidance, and burning daylight—none of which will help you achieve your goal.

Everyone loves the idea of being able to pick the next hot stock, like buying $100 of Amazon at its IPO and it being worth more than $100,000 several decades later. While there are plenty of books, websites, financial advisors, and strangers who claim to have the crystal ball, they don't. Some financial advisors are happy for you to give them control of your money so they can sell you mutual funds with 5.75% upfront commissions and hefty annual maintenance fees. Others will try to sell you whole value life insurance, which will rip your eyes out in fees. When I was in law school, I used to watch a guy on CNBC yell into the camera about his stock recommendations and explain to his audience why they were the next big thing. Two stocks I bought on his recommendation yielded me -80% returns, and a third went to $0. When it comes to investing, I have found that it is exponentially easier to get bad advice than it is to get good advice. Listening to the wrong advice can cost you dearly.

My interest in investing piqued after I realized how poorly I was doing at it and how many years I wasted. After years of following random tidbits of advice from finance articles in magazines and online, talking to friends and relatives, and trying to keep up with market research in my free time, I was grossly underperforming the S&P 500 (i.e., "the market"). I had no strategy whatsoever. My "plan" was to save some money in my retirement account and brokerage account, but not a specific amount every month. I spent 5 minutes looking at the options available to me in my 401(k) but never followed up to monitor performance. The only stocks and mutual funds where I did "well" were ones I selected by chance. For instance, I bought Apple stock at the same time I bought Sears and Blackberry stock; 15 years later, one is the most valuable company in the world, while the others may not even exist as of the day you're reading this book. My big wins offset the big losses.

Here is the hard truth of my journey: it is possible that had I done the right things earlier in my life, I could have saved significantly more for retirement than I have now. Even though I tried to educate myself about investing, I read the wrong articles and listened to the wrong people. For me, it was a classic case of "paralysis by analysis" because I gathered input from so many different sources with so many different strategies, I ended up mostly doing nothing. I missed out on much of the stock market's recovery between 2009 and 2012, a timeframe in which the S&P 500 doubled. Had I invested in a basic index fund that tracked the S&P 500, my returns would have been phenomenal; instead, my lack of a plan led to a below-average performance.

I made the mistake of wasting a good part of my late 20's and will never be able to recoup the growth on that money that would have compounded several times over between now and my retirement date. On the upside, I have learned from my mistakes. I want you to learn from them too.

When it comes to *would've*, *could've*, and *should've* for our respective retirements, you and I—and probably most everyone else—have a lot in common. Your divorce, though, has put you into recovery mode. You have a diminished nest egg and a long road to travel to get to where you anticipated you would be at retirement. You and I cannot afford to spend any more time dwelling on the past, nor can we waste time in the present. Achieving a substantial balance in your retirement account requires you to start doing the right things and taking the right steps beginning today.

Let's cut right to the chase and talk about whose advice you should follow when it comes to investing once you are debt-free. I recommend three experts: Dave Ramsey, Jack Bogle, and J.L. Collins. For the time being, ignore everyone else.

Dave Ramsey tells you to save 15% of your income for retirement; this is an absolute must. It is a simple calculation: whatever your pre-tax gross annual income is, multiply that by 0.15, and then divide by the number of paychecks you receive each year. Adjust your retirement withholdings to put that amount into your 401(k) every paycheck. If you make $70,000 annually, 15% is $10,500 per year or $403.84 per paycheck. Once your mortgage is paid off, you will be able to bolster that amount significantly. However, for now, 15% is suitable because this will leave you money to chip away at your mortgage for an early payoff.

Ramsey advocates paying down your mortgage for several reasons, including the security of a paid-off house and the ability to supercharge your investments once you have eliminated your mortgage payment. While there are plenty of "experts" who will try to convince you that a mortgage is "good debt" because "you can make more money by investing in the stock market," what they fail to acknowledge is human behavior and the value of security. As someone who has paid off his mortgage, I can attest that money that does not have a specific purpose in your budget will get spent. Sure, on paper, if you have $1,500 leftover every month to either throw at your 3.25% mortgage or commit to investing in the stock market, then you will probably get a better return in the market over the long term. However, if that $1,500 looks more like $900 being invested—because you decided to buy a new 60" television, ate out at restaurants, or spent it on a vacation instead of investing it all—the debate is moot.

Every dollar paid toward your mortgage principal reduces your debt, increases your net worth, accelerates your home payoff date, and reduces the amount of interest you pay to the bank over the life of the loan. On a $200,000 home loan on a 30-year fixed-rate mortgage at 3.5%, adding a $1,000 additional principal payment each month pays the loan off 19 years earlier and saves you $84,000 in interest. Also, with your mortgage paid off, your security is vastly different than when you still have to make a monthly payment. Moreover, with no mortgage payment, you can devote a significant amount each month to saving and investing like you have never before experienced.

Finally, if you have children, it is your choice whether you want to pay for some or all of their college education. If you are way behind on your retirement savings, or if your child has selected a school or major that you do not support (such as attending an out-of-state school to pursue a degree in basket weaving), you can decide whether that is the best use of your money. That said, if you are out of debt and you can afford to help, this is the time to set aside money—especially if your children are young. For example, investing $200 per month in a child's college fund for ten years will yield more than $36,000 of tax-free funds at a compounded 8% return. The same amount invested over 18 years at the same return yields $96,000.

For your investment strategy, follow the guidance of Jack Bogle and J.L. Collins.

While I am clearly a fan of Dave Ramsey's get-out-of-debt advice and fully support his plan in Baby Steps #4-6, I believe that Jack Bogle and J.L. Collins compliment his advice with specific guidance on investing and wealth-building that is more comprehensive than is laid out in *The Total Money Makeover*.

Any investor can be overwhelmed by the investment choices available to you. Stocks, bonds, mutual funds, index funds, exchange-traded funds (ETFs), commodities, precious metals, futures, options, money market funds, certificates of deposit, hedge funds, annuities, and real estate investment trusts (REITs) are all vehicles where you can invest. It is easy to lose money if you don't know what you are doing, and also if you think you know exactly what you are doing.

Investing does not have to be complicated.

One of the reasons I advocate the teachings of Jack Bogle and J.L. Collins is that they simplify investing to the point that even someone brand new to it can understand where to invest, how to invest, and why the methodology of investing in index funds is best positioned to achieve results over the long haul.

> *A low-cost index fund is the most sensible equity investment for the great majority of investors.*
>
> **- Warren Buffett, as quoted in Jack Bogle's book, *The Little Book of Common Sense Investing***

Warren Buffett, the CEO and chairman of holding company Berkshire Hathaway, is one of the most successful investors ever. He is nicknamed "The Oracle of Omaha" for his consistently prophetic views on investing and the market. Despite being one of the ten wealthiest people in the world and one of the best stock pickers ever, Buffett is a major proponent of low-cost index funds such as the S&P 500. The S&P 500 is an index that is comprised of the 500 largest companies that are traded on American stock exchanges. It is considered by many to be the best representation of the U.S. stock market. When you hear someone say "the market," it's a safe bet to assume they are referring to the performance of the S&P 500.

In 2007, Buffett was so confident in the S&P 500's ability to outperform actively-managed hedge funds that he made a $1 million bet with a hedge fund manager that the S&P 500 would outperform his opponent's handpicked portfolio of five hedge funds over ten years. Buffett's hypothesis, proven true, was that a low-cost index fund would outperform a portfolio of hedge funds after fees, costs, and expenses. Buffett won handily, with the S&P 500 returning over 85% versus a 22% return from the average of the five hedge funds nine years into the bet before his opponent conceded. [28]

28. David Floyd, *Buffett's Bet with the Hedge Funds: And the Winner Is...*, INVESTORPEDIA, (updated June 25, 2019), https://www.investopedia.com/articles/investing/030916/buffetts-bet-hedge-funds-year-eight-brka-brkb.asp.

***The Little Book of Common Sense Investing* by Jack Bogle is a must-read.**

The best book on index fund investing is written by Jack Bogle, who is the founder of The Vanguard Group—an investment brokerage firm with over $6 trillion in assets under management. Bogle is called the father of index investing because he committed his life to helping people achieve great wealth through investing in low-cost (meaning low fees) index funds. His legacy is carried on through Vanguard, which is known for having some of the lowest fees in the business and being one of the few brokerages owned by its investors.

Index funds are naturally diversified because they are comprised of many companies and not just one company's stock. The S&P 500 index fund covers a myriad of sectors too, so when one sector is down, the index fund can be buoyed by companies and sectors that are up. Also, if a particular company on the index underperforms, it will be booted from the index and replaced by an emerging firm that is performing well.

Bogle's book, *The Little Book of Common Sense Investing: The Only Way to Guarantee Your Fair Share of Stock Market Returns*, convincingly spells out the case for low-cost index funds and passive investing by regularly contributing from every paycheck until you retire. To be successful at picking stocks or actively managed mutual funds that consistently beat the market over the long term, you would have to be in the top 5% of stock pickers and mutual fund managers in the world; this is why Bogle argues that passively investing in low-cost index funds is the right course of action for most regular investors. His book also reveals the incredible impact that fees and expenses can have in diminishing your returns.

Bogle's book should be read as a primer to *The Simple Path to Wealth* by J.L. Collins.

The full title of J.L. Collins' book is *The Simple Path to Wealth: Your Roadmap to Financial Independence and a Rich, Free Life*. I cannot think of a better, more descriptive title for what he teaches in his book. *The Simple Path to Wealth* is very sparse on debt elimination, which makes sense because the only way to achieve financial independence is to be debt-free and stay out of debt. In this regard, *The Total Money Makeover* is a fine primer. Rather, Collins' work does a fantastic job guiding you on what to do money when you are in a position to save and invest, much like Bogle's book.

Bogle's and Collins' respective books are the best one-two punch I have found to educate anyone on investing and wealth-building. **I cannot say it enough: read these books as soon as you put this one down.**

Bogle's book provides the foundation for why you should invest in index funds, while Collins' book epically carries the torch by covering every other aspect of investing and wealth building. He leads a discussion about financial independence, then lays out all of the steps you need to take in order to achieve that goal. His advice will allow you to get started right away and guide you through where you should invest, how you should invest, and strategies to employ through the point that you achieve financial independence.

The Simple Path to Wealth answers virtually every question you could think to ask about the types of accounts to invest in (401(k), 403(b), HSA, Traditional IRA, Roth IRA, etc.), the difference between index funds, mutual funds, and exchange-traded funds (ETFs), recommended brokerages to use, diversification, the case for using a robo-advisor vs. a fiduciary advisor vs. no advisor, retirement withdrawal rates, equities/bonds mixtures based on your age, and so much more. J.L. Collins openly speaks of Jack Bogle being his hero, and his advice in *The Simple Path to Wealth* builds on everything you will read in *The Little Book of Common Sense Investing*, which in my opinion, builds on everything covered in *The Total Money Makeover*.

While you may be sitting there thinking: *"Wait—your advice to me is to pick up not just one, not two, but THREE other books?"*

That is 100% correct.

I would be doing you a disservice if I tried to explain all the teachings of Dave Ramsey, Jack Bogle, and J.L. Collins. I would be sending you out to sea without a compass or map if I gave you a watered-down version of their teachings in my own words. It would be a travesty if I attempted to come up with a better plan than those taught by three of the greatest financial teachers of the last half-century. Instead, I'm sending you straight to the best of the best. This saves you from wasting time that you cannot afford to waste.

More importantly, these books are simple, straightforward, and inspiring. Collectively, they lay out a financial plan that a tenth-grader could understand and offer the most constructive investment advice you could follow regardless of whether you are new to the world of investing or have 30 years of experience.

So, read these books. Follow what they teach. Invest 15% of your gross income for retirement until you have your house paid off. Once you achieve that milestone, you are on the fastest road to not just a total recovery but financial independence.

STAGE THREE:

THE WEALTH ACCUMULATION & PRESERVATION STAGE

When you have no debt whatsoever and you own your residence outright, you can supercharge your savings and investment rate like no other. You should be maxing out your retirement accounts, Health Savings Account (HSA), and every tax-advantaged account available to you. At this point, you should still be on a budget because spending every dollar you bring in will not only deprive you of your ability to retire when you want but also the ability to live the life in retirement that you have long dreamed of living.

I will caution you that with no mortgage and no debt, you are still susceptible to making a big-ticket purchase on credit because you have no other monthly payments to remind you how quickly monthly payments can drain your bank account. If you have thought to yourself, "well, it would *only* be a $500 per month car payment," then you have become numb to the adverse impact that debt will have on your life. While it may be easier to save $30,000 in cash since you have no payments beyond your daily living expenses, property taxes, and utilities, handing over $30,000 to buy a car in cash is still a difficult prospect. The car dealership will try to lure you back into debt by teasing their 0.9% interest rate and "advising" you that putting only $500 down allows you to keep $29,500 in the bank. And that sales pitch may work on you. In other words, you are fully capable of finding yourself right back in Stage One—where you have consumer debt and, therefore, monthly payments on that debt.

Nevertheless, if you have the mindset that you will never go back into debt and that you will pay for your next car, roof replacement, and new HVAC in cash, then I am proud to know you and have zero concerns for your financial future.

The starting point for anyone in Stage Three is the same as to those in Stage Two, which is to read *The Little Book of Common Sense Investing* by Jack Bogle and *A Simple Path to Wealth* by J.L. Collins. However, my advice does not end there.

I would encourage you to keep reading and keep educating yourself. Expanding your knowledge in all areas of personal finance, taxation, and estate planning will help you craft a vision for your future. Use a compounding interest calculator to figure out how much you can expect to have at retirement based upon what you already have saved up, what you intend on saving every month until you retire, and what the numbers would look like if you saved an extra 10% or achieved a slightly lower rate of return.

Read up on retirement withdrawal rates. If you retire at 65, you could conceivably live another 35+ years, and your money needs to last you that long. Read up on social security, when to take it, and what impact that will have on your retirement. Read up on required minimum distributions from your 401k and IRAs. These are all advanced topics, and many are covered in J.L. Collins' *A Simple Path to Wealth*. Yet, the law and regulations are always changing, so your job is to stay up-to-date on the topics that will most impact your financial situation in retirement. Consult professionals if you need to. The cost of a good wills & trusts attorney is peanuts compared to the money that can be preserved for your loved ones and kept out of the government's hands with proper estate planning.

With no debt and no mortgage, you are in a unique position compared to the overwhelming majority of your peers. You do not have the same stress and anxiety as those in debt, nor do you need to pick up extra work to generate more income to maintain your lifestyle. Any additional work or overtime is purely optional for you and is a great financial move because you can gain back a lot of ground lost in your divorce.

From time to time, you may find yourself dwelling on the money you lost in the divorce. I get it. I see it on every client's face when I explain the law to them at our first meeting. Just as I cannot dwell on any bad investment I have made in my life and every bull market I have missed, you cannot dwell on something that you cannot change. What you can change is your savings rate, and what you can control are your lifestyle, your spending, your investment choices, and your retirement.

As discussed in Part I, compounding interest is your greatest ally. Every year that you have left until retirement, and every year that you can live in retirement without touching your nest egg, represents an opportunity to reap the awesome benefit of compound interest. When you educate yourself on topics such as when to take social security and the amount you can comfortably withdrawal in retirement once you stop working, you can come up with a game plan in advance so it is not a rushed decision.

Finally, if you are still working, now is the time to plan for what your day-to-day life is going to look like in retirement. Are you going to start a new career, start a small business, volunteer, or pursue a hobby? Chris Hogan, the author of the best-selling book *Retire Inspired: It's Not an Age, It's a Financial Number*, encourages his audience to "dream in HD (AKA high-definition)." His thesis is that, just like planning for any other long-term goal, the more you define the goal, the better your odds of hitting it. Putting specificity to your retirement plans will give you an idea of exactly how much you will need to have saved to live the retirement of your dreams. You can adjust your retirement date and contributions based upon your returns.

Financial independence can be achieved through intentionality and following a plan. If you follow the guidance of the experts endorsed in this book, you too can achieve a full recovery from your divorce and greater financial success. Any financial setback you have endured in your life is behind you. You have survived one of the most taxing things any of us can ever experience and come out strong on the other side. With the level of grit, determination, and focus that led you to this point of being debt-free and having a paid-off house, I am fully confident in your ability to keep working towards financial independence. I am happy to pass the torch to Jack Bogle and J.L. Collins to show you how to achieve that goal.

While you work to achieve financial independence, you can help so many people through the generous giving of your time and money. Your wealth will allow you to change your life, the lives of your children and grandchildren, and strangers, friends, acquaintances, and organizations you choose to bless through your financial support.

At some point, you will achieve a full financial recovery from your divorce. The concept of a "recovery" is a bit abstract and therefore it is tough to define. It may not be hitting a specific number in your bank and retirement accounts, but rather achieving a mindset of peace. I hope that one day, you will be in such a fantastic financial position that you wake up from a peaceful night's sleep and realize that you have no worries about your finances, no anxiety about the amount you have saved for retirement, and harbor no negative emotions from the rocky road you traveled after your divorce.

When you get to that point, be sure to reach out to me through my website at *MikeJurek.com* and share your story. I look forward to hearing from you. Until then, I wish you the best of luck on your journey.

PART III:

GUIDANCE FOR THE MEMBERS OF THE SUPPORT NETWORK

For Parts I and II of this book, I have used the term *you* to speak directly to divorcees. From here on out, I am speaking to *you*—the kind-hearted member of a support network who is spending your free time reading this book because there is someone in your life who you care so deeply about you want to help them financially recover from one of life's most devastating events. Despite all your love and good intentions, your efforts may not be met with gratitude from the person you are trying to help. I will thank you on their behalf because, without you, your loved one might have to put their life back together all alone.

Some divorce attorneys shudder at the thought of their clients' mothers and fathers, brothers and sisters, friends, and coworkers being peripherally involved in the divorce process because of the contrary advice they may offer. At times I share this sentiment. Nevertheless, more often, I am glad my clients have a strong support network involved in their lives during the divorce because they almost always back the common-sense and pragmatic advice I offer. Having my clients' closest allies reaffirm my guidance, in their own words, is helpful because it reinforces what I believe to be best for their cases and their lives.

Ultimately, my role is that of a hired deckhand who has more in common with you and the other members of your loved one's support network than I do with my client, who is captaining the ship. I remind my clients all the time that they are the ones who must make the final decisions, and they have the final say on how we proceed. In this regard, I am no different than you; I offer my input, but it may or may not be followed by the person I am trying to help.

The words of guidance that follow are based on my experiences in helping hundreds of people navigate through some of the roughest periods in their lives. Since everyone's situation is different, it is impossible to tell if my suggestions will be helpful or not to you as you try to assist in your loved one's recovery. You, however, are the x-factor. You are clearly interested in helping your loved one as much as you can because you have made it this far, and I know for a fact that nobody is reading this book for fun. I hope that, at the very minimum, you will feel empowered and educated as you attempt to accompany them in their financial endeavors.

We are all capable of giving bad advice.

Nobody thinks "*I give bad advice.*" We all think, in the moment, that our guidance is the best course of action. But since we're human, we're all capable of providing poor guidance sometimes. Looking back with 20/20 hindsight, the times I gave bad advice were because one or more of the following occurred:

- I spoke about a subject on which I thought I was fully educated but was not;
- I did not have all the facts;
- I spoke from a place of emotion rather than a place of reason; and/or
- I did a poor job of communicating my opinion, and so it was misinterpreted by the recipient.

These are common mistakes that any of us can easily make. You must try to avoid these missteps for your input to be of any value to whoever is listening.

You do not have to be an expert, but you *must* be educated on the subject matter.

I am not a mental health expert. Outside of taking a Psychology 101 class in college, I have no training whatsoever in mental health. Though as a divorce attorney, I am certainly exposed to clients and counterparts who have mental health issues, but since I am not formally educated in the field, I refer my clients to experts who are credentialed and therefore in a position to provide legitimate advice and treatment. Similarly, although you do not need to be a financial wizard to help guide your loved one post-divorce, you do need to be educated and someone who practices good money habits.

In Part I, we reviewed the financial mistakes that ensnare countless divorcees every year. Part II covers the get-out-of-debt and personal finance authors and plans that I advocate divorcees follow to achieve financial success. I can only assume that you are reading this book because you are concerned about your loved one's handling of finances—which may include one or more of the mistakes identified in Part I, or the absence of any sort of plan like that discussed in Part II.

While I understand and admire your desire to speak up, I must caution you of the following: **If you want to help your loved one walk the journey to financial recovery, BUT your finances are a mess and you are NOT taking any steps to improve your financial situation, you should not offer any sort of financial guidance to your loved one.**

As an adult, you get to decide how you live your life. When it comes to your finances, you decide how you are going to spend your money and if you are going to save any of it. The plan advocated in this book for divorcees to follow, as you read in Parts I and II, includes a strict anti-debt attitude that you may not share. You may be opposed to the idea of living on a budget in your own life and may believe there is nothing wrong with borrowing money to buy big things like a car or smaller items like appliances and furniture.

Nevertheless, if you are going to be an accountability partner for someone who is walking the journey of eliminating debt, you—as a confidant—will be a destructive force in their recovery if you undermine the principles of the path mapped out in this book and the recommended follow-up resources. Statements like "*there's nothing wrong with borrowing money to buy a reliable car*" or "*you don't have to be shackled by a budget to get out of debt*" are in direct contradiction to your loved one's journey. As a crude comparison, those statements are akin to telling someone who is working the Alcoholics Anonymous steps that it is okay to have one drink. If you plan to contribute your own contrary opinions, like these, then you are the wrong person to be an accountability partner and should not serve a role in your loved one's financial recovery. You would be better off giving this book to your loved one as a gift instead, picking up the tab whenever you two go out for dinner, and discussing every aspect of your lives other than your respective finances whenever you spend time together.

To be helpful as an accountability partner—and, more importantly, as a companion on your loved one's journey to financial recovery—you do not need to be perfect with your finances. In fact, since the invention of currency, no person has ever existed who has been perfect with money in their own life. But to be helpful and effective, you must be educated and a cheerleader of the process that is outlined in this book. If you do not have your financial affairs in order but still want to help, then my advice to you is to start walking the same journey as your loved one.

To me, the best part of the get-out-of-debt plan taught by Dave Ramsey, the investment advice of Jack Bogle, and the guidance of J.L. Collins is that anyone can follow what they teach. I wrote this book as a supplement to the most popular "get-out-of-debt" educational materials available because I found most writings on the subject to be aimed at married couples and individuals who are not starting over following a life-altering event such as divorce. However, divorcees are walking a markedly different journey than everyone else, albeit toward the same destination of financial independence. A divorcee starting over and facing a mountain of debt is vastly different than someone right out of college facing a mountain of student loan debt. Sure, both individuals will have to work the program with a similar level of dedication and sacrifice, but I am convinced that the divorcee has a much rockier road to travel due to the emotional turmoil they are facing.

The beauty of the plan outlined in Part II is that anyone can take the same steps, engage in the same intentional behavior, and find success with money. Regardless of whether the plan is worked by an individual or a married couple, it works when the steps are followed precisely as they are presented. That includes you too.

Your heart may be in a good place, but it is hypocritical to try and coach someone on how to be good with money if you are not taking any steps to be responsible with it yourself. I am not suggesting that you have to be a millionaire or diehard follower of the Ramsey plan to offer advice, but you do need to be on a budget, living within your means, opposed to taking on debt of any kind, and generally following the same steps that are advocated herein. If you are not living on a budget, or you have a lackadaisical attitude toward debt, you will be limited in your ability to help your loved one walk this journey.

So, if you want to help but are unsure where to start, get yourself on the same plan. Part II of this book is just as applicable to you too, as are the supplemental resources I recommend.

I have led *Financial Peace University* classes out of my law office for years, and each session has been valuable to me in my debt-free journey. I openly speak about my mistakes, wins, losses, and the overall lessons I have learned because I am making the same trek towards financial independence as those in the class. If you truly want to help your loved one but your finances are a mess, one of the best things you can do is be transparent about how things are going for you, including your progress and any setbacks you've encountered as you walk this journey. It is like joining a gym with your friend; you each have your own goals and different starting points, but if you both work at it, stick to a regular schedule, and hold each other accountable, you will both see results.

Read the same materials I recommended in Parts I and II so you know and understand the lessons the experts are teaching your loved one. This way, you will be able to speak the same language and use the same terminology. Similarly, listen to the same podcasts as your loved one and use the lessons you learn from these resources in your discussions. Learning via these books and podcasts will empower you to talk intelligently about the various aspects of personal finance, including budgeting, saving, investing, and the methodology of the Baby Steps, all while commiserating about the struggles of behavior modification, sacrifice, and setbacks along the way.

You can't expect your loved one to be an open book about their finances unless you share some pages out of yours.

Several years ago, a friend of mine revealed to me, in confidence, that he and his wife had over $180,000 in student loan debt. He had just graduated from law school and had financed his entire undergraduate and graduate education. His student loan debt exceeded what he owed on his house. He was stressed and anxious because he and his wife had no plan to tackle his student loan debt. In other words, they were "normal."

I told him to bring his wife to the *Financial Peace University* classes I was leading. Thankfully for him and his marriage, they followed through. They attended the nine-week course and have stuck with the program for the past year and a half. As of the publication of this book, he and his wife have paid off more than $110,000 in student loan debt and have plans to extinguish the remaining amount within the next two years.

Thanks to the initial openness of our personal finance discussions, our friendship has grown to the point where we now talk honestly about all aspects of our financial lives. There are virtually no topics about our finances that are off-limits. We know each other's salaries, bonuses, raises, levels of debt, mortgage interest rates, investment amounts, retirement amounts, and the ways in which we have both controlled our spending. He and I have an open dialogue about the finances of our respective households that is more transparent than most anyone else in my life besides my financial advisor. Being candid and trusting each other has been invaluable for both of us on our journeys.

In talking to my colleague and his wife, I realized at the outset of our discussions that for me to be an effective communicator and coach, I needed to know the depths of the hole they were in and size of their shovel for them to dig themselves out. I could not expect him and his wife to open up and reveal the monsters hiding in their closet unless I was willing to be open about my own struggles and situation too. Once our respective debts were revealed, we naturally started to discuss our incomes and spending habits too. Simply stated, we could not talk about saving without sharing details, and we could not talk about timelines for debt-payoff goals without telling each other how much debt we each had.

Having the complete financial picture is a must, but getting there takes time.

Whenever I act as a financial coach or divorce attorney, I need to know about every single debt, asset, and source of income. Without this information, I cannot give appropriate advice. When I wear a professional hat, people tend to be open and honest with me because they view me as a professional who they've come to for advice. That relationship has the advantage of a built-in level of trust that assumes confidentiality; of course, as an attorney, the attorney-client privilege is sacrosanct. More importantly, I am able to get direct answers and the full financial picture often in a few minutes with a handful of direct questions.

On the other hand, when I wear the hat of a friend who is trying to help another friend with their finances, there isn't an immediate assumption of trust—despite the longevity of our friendship—simply because it is so rare in our society for people to openly discuss things like their income, debt, and net worth. As a result, whereas my divorce clients and students know nothing about my finances, the opposite is true when it comes to my friends. I usually have to divulge more personal details in order to bring the conversation to a place where they themselves are comfortable sharing details too.

Although it is easier said than done, in order to truly help, you must know the depths of your loved one's financial hole. You need to know their income, expenses, budget, and whether they are sticking to their budget or not. You can only be an accountability partner if you see the budget to which you are holding them accountable. That level of transparency may not be immediate. If you find yourself dealing with such a dynamic, you will likely have to share some details about your own situation to get the conversation going. You do not have to disclose your net worth, income, or account balances, but general information about your budget, your money struggles, effective strategies you have used, and frugality tips are all things you should expect to discuss.

Your advice must be grounded in logic, not emotion.

As a longtime greater Cincinnati resident, I can honestly say that I would be a horrible play-by-play radio commentator for the Cincinnati Bengals football team—which has not won a playoff game since January 1991. Most people do not realize that the team, not the broadcast network, selects and employs its own local radio commentators.

Given my frustrated fandom at watching lackluster performances on the field for the last few decades, I would be unable to make it through the broadcast without criticizing the coaching, play calls, product on the field, and ownership because I would be speaking with raw emotion. Despite the prestige and presumably hefty paycheck, I am fairly certain that years of pent-up frustration as a fan—and my emotional and visceral responses to blunders on the field—would lead me to be the first NFL play-by-play announcer fired mid-game and likely in the first half of play. When it comes to the Bengals, my emotions would inevitably overpower my rationality.

By the same token, I dislike the thought of handling a heated divorce for one of my best friends or family members because I am too close to the situation, which may result in my advice, strategy, and advocacy being subconsciously influenced by emotion. I have handled dissolutions for friends but not knock-down, drag-out litigation. I have always referred friends whose marriages have ended contentiously to other attorneys. This is the same reason why doctors shouldn't treat their own family members except under extraordinary and limited circumstances—the x-factor for emotionally-influenced judgment exists when it is literally absent in every other case.

In my opinion, one of the least desirable traits in an attorney is when they treat their clients' problems as if they are their own. I deal with attorneys all the time who act as if the court is determining the custody of their own children. While an outsider may perceive this as passion, in the courtroom, it often plays out like a train wreck.

In divorce cases, my role as a trial lawyer is to direct the court to the evidence that exists through witnesses and exhibits. I must be prepared to show my client's best evidence while explaining away anything contrary. Seasoned trial lawyers will tell you that litigants frequently downplay their misdeeds. As such, every time a client tells me a story, I naturally press them on the facts while they sit in my conference room so I can see if the story holds up or if it has weaknesses that will assuredly get exposed in the courtroom. I would rather learn about my client's weaknesses at that point than being blindsided in the courtroom.

I have found over time that attorneys who are too emotionally involved tend to believe that their clients' stories are bulletproof and as a result can have a blind spot to contrary evidence. Such a mindset can lead to the attorney being surprised in the courtroom because they did not preemptively press their client ahead of time for weaknesses and inconsistencies in their story. This often leads to the client is getting lit up on cross-examination, all while the attorney sits there helpless and surprised to learn the other side of the story.

The longer you have known someone and the stronger your relationship, the greater the possibility that you will be emotionally invested in their situation. When your outlook comes from a place of emotion, your advice has the risk of being tainted in the same way emotion impacts a surgeon's ability to operate on her own child or my ability to call play-by-play for a Bengals football game.

Therefore, if you want to help someone on their road to financial recovery following a divorce, you cannot say or do things that will stoke either of your emotions. Some examples of this are rehashing the lowlights of the relationship, the amount of debt your loved one is responsible for repaying, the misdeeds of their ex-spouse, and the "unfair" amount of support ordered by the court. Any mention of the ex-spouse's name should not include an expletive adjective either. These kinds of statements steer the conversation away from the rational and directly into the emotional. While your loved one's ex may have created the mess, the amount of child/spousal support may seem unfair, and the ex may indeed be worthy of an unfavorable moniker, any discussion of these things will just stoke the emotional fire.

Conversely, if your loved one keeps trying to vent to you, there is certainly a time and place for that. The wrong time is at the regular budget meeting; the right time may be over dinner or a drink when you're not trying to solve money problems rationally. One way to handle this is by kindly asking: "Do you want me to listen to you vent, or should we talk about finances?"

Sometimes it is necessary to listen to the venting before your advice can be heard, so separate the two. It is also possible your loved one may not be in the position to accept any advice if they are too emotionally charged so your financial conversation may have to wait a day.

When you are trying to support someone during or after their divorce, you will undoubtedly see them experience the ups and downs of the emotional rollercoaster. It is painful to see a loved one struggle. You must stay strong; you cannot advocate something that will temporarily alleviate their emotional pain but hamstring their financial recovery. A common example of this is your loved one spending beyond their budget as a form of retail therapy, as discussed in detail in Part I. If they spent $150 on clothes when only $40 was budgeted for the month—and you are the accountability partner—your job will be difficult when they start trying to justify the deviation from the plan. It is a delicate situation, but one you must be prepared to endure.

When it comes to the budget, a purchase is binary—it is either within the budget parameters or it is not. If you green-light slip-ups, you are enabling your loved one and failing in your role as an accountability partner. To truly be an accountability partner and effectively serve in the role of being an aid instead of an enabler, you cannot approve of expenditures that are not in the budget, regardless of the justifications offered to you. A sponsor would certainly not give their approval to an alcoholic who offered the same excuse to justify taking a drink. If you buy into the excuse, you allow your emotions to trump the rational part of your brain that knows that the only way your loved one is going to get out of debt is to stick to the budget.

The better response is to look at the budget, determine where other allocations can be adjusted, and build in a "bad day" envelope if emotional spending is a routine problem. An earmarked, nominal amount of money set aside for your loved one to carelessly or frivolously spend each month could be necessary. By helping your loved one prepare for the next emotional flare-up, you will remove the emotional justifications from the equation and mitigate the potential for long-term harm that can be caused by impulse purchases.

When slip-ups occur, don't delay talking about them; address them right away. Discuss the cause, the emotions your loved one felt at the time, how they feel now (to see if they learned anything from it), and brainstorm ways to ensure that it will not happen again. You must address mistakes without levying judgment or guilt because deviations are going to happen. This is precisely why accountability partners are necessary—to hold the person accountable to their budget. Your job is not to scold or shame; it is to help, educate, and inspire. Use these lapses in judgment as learning experiences and a reason to reexamine and modify the budget as needed. The last thing you want is for your loved one to start hiding slip-ups from you. If that happens, you will never have all the information you need to give useful advice.

If you find yourself admonishing the person you are trying to help for failing to stick to the plan, this means that your emotions have trumped your rationality. As the voice of reason, and with the full understanding that getting on a budget and adhering to it can be very difficult, you can assuredly expect growing pains, frustration, and noncompliance by the person you are trying to help. Part I of this book should remind you that the journey you signed up for is a long one since financial recovery may take years to achieve. As a result, if you are going to involve yourself, be prepared to go the distance and resist the temptation to express disappointment at the occasional setback.

When faced with a question you cannot immediately answer, do not risk giving the wrong answer; instead, find the right answer.

If you are new to being an accountability partner, there will be plenty of things that you do not know and have never before encountered. Nobody knows everything about personal finance, and you are not expected to know everything to be an effective companion in this journey. Nevertheless, there will be times when you are unable to offer advice because you do not readily have the answer. Do not guess; take your time and do some research to find the answer so you do not accidentally steer your loved one in the wrong direction. *"Let me get back to you on that"* is a perfectly acceptable answer to a challenging question that you still need to research.

As noted in Part II, one of the reasons I advocate Dave Ramsey's methodology for getting out of debt is because he and his team have covered almost every issue imaginable and have likely published an article, YouTube video, radio show segment, or book chapter that provides the answer to your question. Again, a simple Google search for "Dave Ramsey" and your question will yield you an instant answer that you will be able to share with your loved one.

Communication is not a one-way street.

I tend to be an open book with my friends and family. Not everyone shares my willingness to discuss almost any subject, including personal finances and debt. Part of my openness comes from what I do daily as a divorce lawyer. During the first ten minutes of my initial consultation with a prospective divorce client, I ask them about their salary, their spouse's salary, their debts, the amount of equity in their home, and what led them to need the services of a divorce lawyer. I cannot think of a more intrusive set of questions outside of those asked in a doctor's office, but my job requires that I ask each within minutes of shaking someone's hand for the first time. I have asked these questions so many times now that I have become somewhat desensitized to the social norms of *not* talking about personal finances, debt, and relational issues.

In leading *Financial Peace University* classes out of my law office over a number of years, I have learned that the more I share about my struggles, the more willing the students in my class are to open up and share their own stories. To get the conversation going, I talk about the dumb things I have done with money. I tell my students about the time in 2011, in an effort to save a few bucks, when I bought concert tickets off of Craigslist to take a girl on a date—only to find out at the gate that the tickets were counterfeit and I had been ripped off. (Fortunately, the woman I took to the concert understood I had good intentions and ended up marrying me a year and a half later.) In 2013, even though I had the money for a down payment on a house, I had to finance a riding lawnmower to cut the acre of land I had bought because I didn't have $1,500 to buy it outright. Try filling out a Sears credit application to buy a Craftsman yard tractor without having Jeff Foxworthy's *you might be a redneck* jokes come to mind. I also have no qualms about telling my students about the stocks I bought that lost almost all of their value or any of the other dumb things I've done with money in the past. My ice-breaker technique gets the discussion going because it underscores the message that nobody has a perfect track-record with money, and the best we can hope for is to learn from our mistakes and do better in the future.

I talk candidly with both strangers and friends alike about all of the ways I have been ripped off and the regrettable money mistakes I have made as a lead-in to then talk about what I have done to take control of my finances. Time and time again, I have found that once I remove the element of embarrassment that accompanies making a bad financial decision, being in a bad financial spot, and just being dumb with money, others are more than willing to share because they do not feel like they are going to be judged.

My clients often tell me when they feel judged by their friends, family members, coworkers, and acquaintances. One would think that in a society with a nearly 50% divorce rate, judgment from the peanut gallery would not be an issue. Yet, it seems impossible for my clients to go through their divorces without experiencing a *fear* of being judged by others. Some of the most difficult conversations one can have in life are born out of divorce. There is certainly an emotional toll that accompanies having to explain to your family that your marriage is over, to your neighbors why you are selling your house, to your Human Resources representative at work why you are changing your health insurance coverage and beneficiary designations, to your coworkers why you are no longer wearing your wedding ring, and to your friends that you shared in common with your ex-spouse why you are no longer together. It is downright exhausting to even think about all feelings these conversations evoke. The act of putting on a brave face and having all of these unenviable conversations is damn near herculean.

For you to successfully communicate with someone who is going through a divorce or recovering from one, you need to establish a level of trust that is built on a foundation of confidential and judgment-free conversations. As such, I suggest reassuring your loved one of the following at the beginning of your journey together:

1. You are there to help in any way you can.
2. Whatever is said will be kept confidential.
3. There is absolutely no reason ever to feel embarrassed or ashamed.
4. You will walk alongside them in this journey the entire way and won't bail on them.

If there is any concern on their part that you're going to immediately share what they say with your spouse when you get home that evening, they won't feel comfortable discussing personal issues with you. Similarly, if the person opening up to you is afraid you will judge them, condemn their personal choices, or stick your nose in the air in disgust, then you can expect your conversations to go nowhere. Also, if you plan to truly be there for them, this means being there for the long haul. They will inevitably make dumb financial mistakes along the way, and if you bail on them for a retail therapy slip-up or something similar, your sudden departure will end up being detrimental in the long run. So, if any of these issues are a problem for you, the truth is that you cannot expect to play a significant role in your loved one's financial recovery, and you would be better off serving them in some other role.

The depth of your dialogue may be partly dependent on your relationship type.

Some people have the kind of relationship with their parents or siblings where they feel they can share everything with them, while others keep their family members at arms-length because they don't want them to know the depths of their troubles. Some will share things with their family that they would never tell their best friend, while others will happily discuss every intimate detail of their life with a bartender but not with anyone from their bloodline.

Due to the attorney-client privilege, my clients generally open up to me because they know what they share with me will be held in strict confidence. I have had clients emphatically tell me that their parents must never find out how much credit card debt they have racked up or that they were the one in the marriage who cheated—not the other way around as they have led their parents to believe.

Sometimes people are willing to trust outsiders more than they are willing to trust those in their inner circle. You may think that your coworker, who is having a difficult time recovering from her divorce, has plenty of family and friends to help her out since she is always posting pictures with her loved ones on social media and has an office covered with pictures of all the people in her life. It is quite possible, however, that she does not feel comfortable talking with any of them about her divorce. Ask any bartender or hairdresser about the kinds of things people share with them; not surprisingly, they have heard it all. Conversely, the lifelong bond you share with your brother doesn't automatically mean he is ever going to deeply discuss his divorce with you in terms of where his marriage went wrong, the financial hole he is in, or the emotions he is experiencing.

Taking all of this into consideration, the type of relationship you have with your loved one may play a heavy hand in the level of openness you experience when you try to broach subjects like debt and spending. If you have always treated your adult children as children, you cannot expect them to have an open dialogue with you the same way they can with a non-judgmental peer. If you have been a gossipy friend, you cannot expect your friends to forget your history of sharing other people's secrets when you try to get them to open up to you. And if you have been a judgmental sibling who never misses an opportunity to say *"I told you so,"* you have a relationship to restore before you can talk to your sibling about such deep topics.

I bring all this up because being present for someone who is either going through a divorce or recovering from one means attaining a level of trust that will not develop overnight if it does not already exist, even if you have a decades-long kinship. Remember, your loved one recently cut off all relational ties with the person who stood by their side at the altar, promised to be there in good times and bad, and pledged all of their worldly possessions in front of their closest family members and friends. Their reluctance to trust others is certainly understandable, and that includes you despite the length of your relationship. Establishing any trusting relationship at this stage in their life may be difficult for them.

> *Nobody cares how much you know until they know how much you care.*
>
> **– Theodore Roosevelt**

Trust is only going to be built with time, regular interaction, and adherence to your promises of confidentiality, the withholding of judgment, and continued availability. It may take months of regular interactions to get to a point where you can achieve in-depth discussions about anything of substance, such as finances. Nevertheless, despite your best efforts and desire to help, you may never get there.

Your loved one may never confide in you the way you want them to. That is okay. If your role is to be the always-present cheerleader watching from the sidelines, that may be all that is needed from you. The people who line the streets of a marathon and cheer the runners who pass by provide a morale boost to those engaged in the grueling race.

Despite all of this, if you feel called to help, do not let the awkwardness of those early conversations stand in the way of expressing your concern about your loved one's well-being, your desire to be present, and your willingness to serve in any role in which you are needed. If they need a shoulder to cry on, be willing to play this role. If they need you to be the plus-one to go to a concert or event so they don't have to go alone, step up. This is what a good friend would do anyway. So long as you are not enabling any bad behavior, honor the role your loved one wants you to play.

———●———

Recognize the difference between being a supporter and an enabler.

There are clear and obvious ways in which your role might devolve into being an enabler instead of a supporter. Take the obvious example of a friend who is recovering from a divorce and always asks you to join them when they go to the bar or the casino to play blackjack—is it a one-time offer, or does the request happen every other day? There is a difference between occasionally going out socially with a friend and normalizing frequent destructive behavior that happens on a regular basis.

A more complicated example is when your loved one starts talking about making a big purchase on something like a new car because it will make them "feel better." If you stand idly by and watch them make a bad financial decision—all premised upon it bringing them temporary joy despite their overall financial health—you risk enabling bad behavior.

Using the phrase "*I am concerned that…*" is an effective way to broach a topic with a friend without coming across as judgmental and preachy. For instance, you can say:

> *Andy, I'm glad you're enthusiastic about the car. It is great to hear some excitement in your voice. I'm a bit*

concerned, though, that this car you want is a hefty undertaking that may stretch you too thin. Remember when you told me last week about how hard it has been for you to make ends meet with your child support payments and credit cards? I worry that adding a car payment on top of that isn't going to make things any easier. I want you to be happy. And I love that you're feeling enthusiastic about anything. I just want to make sure, as your friend, that the thing that excites you now isn't going to be a burden on you once the enthusiasm fades away.

In Part I, I told you about the difficulty I regularly experience when I talk to clients about things like their house, car, and RV that they cannot "afford" post-divorce. You having that conversation can be ten times more difficult. In Andy's case, the "low" monthly payments spread out over seven years may make the car seem "affordable" to him, but you know from talking with him over the past few months that his finances are a mess. There are better ways to handle the situation than saying "*you can't afford that!*" because the finance manager at the dealership has spread the loan out over so many years that he has convinced Andy that he can indeed handle that "low" payment.

Your goal is to be supportive without enabling bad decisions. Saying to Andy, "*that's great, man!*" and encouraging him to do whatever is going to make him temporarily happy, despite recognizing the financial ramifications he will face because of the decision, would make you an enabler. As a confidant, the best you can do is offer your concern. You have an outside perspective and can remind your loved one that you have their best interests in mind, unlike the car salesperson trying to make a commission.

Using the phrase, "*I am concerned that…*" does exactly what you want it to do—it expresses your concern about their behavior. It does not insult their intelligence or threaten the friendship. At the end of the day, all you can do is try because your loved one is an adult who will ultimately do whatever they want despite your best efforts.

Lending money will change your relationship.

As a close supporter of your loved one during their financial recovery, you may find yourself being asked to lend money. Please, for the sake of your relationship, don't do it. If you want to help and are in a financial position to do so, gift the money or simply decline the request. Without reservation, I will emphatically tell you never to lend your friends or family members money unless *dire* and *extraordinary* circumstances call for it, such as to help them avoid bankruptcy or foreclosure. I hesitate even to give that exception because the person asking to borrow money will likely pitch their situation as "dire" when it most likely is not.

When you lend money, you change the dynamic between you and your loved one, creating a borrower/lender situation. As the Bible reminds us, "the borrower is a slave to the lender."[29] I have made the mistake of lending money to a friend in need, and I hope you can learn from that mistake.

In 2014, I tried to do a favor for a friend by selling him my car at a discount and allowing him to pay a manageable $100 per month. My car had a Blue Book value of $2,500, was reliable, and had plenty of life left. I was going to sell it because I was ready for an upgrade. My friend needed a car for his wife so she could

---

29. Proverbs 22:7.

finish her nursing degree. Although he had a full-time job as an accountant, he was strapped for cash because he was paying his wife's tuition and she had no income. Naturally, he expected their financial situation to improve once she was done with school and gainfully employed. They were in a bind because the car she was driving was leased, and the lease was up at the end of the month. I learned all of this at a mutual friend's dinner party and felt a desire to help them as best as I could. I figured that selling the car to him at a discount would get him and his wife out of a bind.

The terms of the deal were simple: my friend would pay me a total of $1,400 by making payments of $100 per month for 14 months. I signed the title over so he could get it insured in his name. He made the first three payments on time, but then the checks stopped coming. I did not call or text him to ask why he wasn't paying but figured that money was tight for whatever reason and trusted that he would make good on our agreement. After the fourth month of no payment, I reached out to him.

I sent him a text message wishing him well, asking if everything was okay, and saying that I felt embarrassed to have to bring to his attention that he was four months behind on his obligation to me. I told him that he could just start paying the $100 per month again and everything would be fine. He quickly responded with an apology and said that money was indeed tight but that he would set up automatic payments from his checking account so there would be no more missed payments. Coincidentally, that same day, his wife posted pictures on Facebook from their week-long trip to Disney World.

He ended up paying the entire balance and never missed another payment. Besides the one text message, I have never said anything to him about it, and to this day we have never discussed it. Yet, although this happened more than five years ago, I know that he is still embarrassed by the entire situation, and I feel bad that he feels that way. The fact that his embarrassment still lingers is why I have regrets over the entire situation. It introduced an element within our friendship that had never before existed. What I intended to be a favor for a friend in need turned out to be a relationship-altering decision on my part. If I had the opportunity to do it again, I would have either gifted him the car or kept my mouth shut and sold the car on Craigslist.

> *Lending money to a friend often results in a twofold loss: both money and friend are gone forever.*
>
> **– W.H. Milburn**

When it comes to stories about lending to friends or family gone wrong, my car sale fiasco is a mild example. I am sure that you have heard horror stories of relationships being ruined and families being divided because of money being lent and not repaid. Learn from my mistake because the last thing you want is to harm your relationship with your loved one, especially when something minor could possibly turn into something major. Even worse, as someone who your loved one is leaning on for support and guidance as they try to navigate life post-divorce, your role in their life is of the utmost importance now more than ever.

Either gift the money (only if you can and only if you want to) or just say no.

If you are asked to lend money to a loved one, I would almost guarantee that the dynamic of your relationship will change as long as the debt is outstanding and possibly beyond. Lending money creates an awkward paradigm where your loved one (the borrower) can't be forthright with you (the lender) about their spending. Here is how it will happen:

Against your better judgment, you lend your longtime friend and coworker $2,000 because she is recovering from a divorce and claims that she needs money right away to make her rent and car payments and to buy groceries for her kids. The two of you agree that she can pay you back $500 per paycheck over the next four paychecks.

Before this financial arrangement, she had no reason to lie to you about her finances or spending. The first paycheck comes, and she makes good on her promise. Before the second payment is due, she asks you if she can pay $250 for the next two paychecks because she has to get her car repaired. You agree. Before you created a debtor/lender relationship, you paid little attention to how she spent her earnings. That changes when she again asks to extend the payoff timeframe; you start to notice that she always has a Starbucks cup in her hand when she comes into work. While you pack your lunch every day, she goes out for lunch. You realize that your repayment is being delayed because she is spending the money that she owes you at restaurants and coffee shops all over town.

In this hypothetical situation, it would be impossible for you not to feel a bit resentful. You were willing to extend your coworker grace, but your relationship may forever be changed if you feel like your kindness was taken advantage of by the very person you set out to help.

A small loan has the potential to damage any relationship permanently. This happens all the time. While it may initially seem counterintuitive, the best thing you can do to preserve your relationship—when faced with a request to lend money—is to either: (1) gift the money if you are in a position to do so and want to do so, or (2) politely decline the request. If the answer is no, then you just need to say no.

> *The holy passion of friendship is of so sweet and steady and loyal and enduring in nature that it will last through a whole lifetime, if not asked to lend money.*
>
> **- Mark Twain**

If you go the gift route, it is reasonable to have strings attached to the gift, so long as it does not involve the repayment of money. After all, it makes no sense to "give a drunk a drink" or enable the continuation of bad behavior. For instance, if you want to help your loved one but are concerned that he is wasting money and not living on a budget, a condition of your generosity may be that he needs to get on a budget and stick to it for one or two months before you hand over the check. Yet, as with any gift, there is a risk that it will not be used in the way you wished it was used; you have to accept that your loved one may be irresponsible with the money and may spend it in a way that is contrary to your wishes.

If you are not in a position to gift the money, or if you simply do not want to gift the money, then you have to be unequivocal in saying no. If you are vague, you leave the door open for repeated requests and plenty of uncomfortable conversations. Remember that "No." is a complete sentence. If you are unwilling or unable to say no outright, feel free to use any of these explanations:

- *Sorry, but I have debts of my own that I need to clean up.*

- *I wish I could, but I don't have any room in my budget.*

- *I'm not able to lend you any money, but I can help you with your budget, list things for sale, find you extra work, and babysit if you want to pick up extra shifts.*

You have to be firm in your response so you don't give any false hope that all you need is more convincing. If you are asked in a high-pressure situation—such as in front of other family members or friends (who have no qualms about giving away your money)—or under highly-emotional circumstances where tears are flowing, then do not feel pressured to say yes, only to try to retract it later. Rather, the following response is appropriate:

- *Let me think about it. I'll let you know tomorrow.*

By saying that you need a day to think it over, you remove yourself from an intense situation where you may feel pressured into saying yes. Instead, you will be able to deliver your position without the same level of emotion or the spotlight that could have otherwise led to you making a decision that is contrary to your better judgment.

Never co-sign for the debt of another.

While lending money should almost always be avoided, co-signing should **always** be avoided. **Never EVER be a co-signer.** When you co-sign a car loan, student loan, residential lease, mortgage, or any debt of another, you are legally obligated for the debt as if it is your debt. This has the potential to go wrong in every way imaginable and in ways you cannot even imagine.

Lenders require co-signers when the primary loan applicant is unable to qualify for a loan on their own. So, when a second person puts their name on the debt, the lender views the loan as less risky because two people can be sued if the debt is not repaid.

Therefore, if someone is in the position that a co-signer is required to get the loan or apartment in the first place, it means the lender or landlord has already determined that the applicant is not worthy of approval on their own due to their lack of income or a lack of a positive history showing an ability to make on-time payments for other debts. In other words, the lender has already decided that the person is too risky for the loan and likely to default on it. That is a major red flag not only for the lender but for you as well.

To see how this can go wrong, let's consider the previously-discussed situation of lending $2,000 to your friend at work. When you lend someone a set amount of cash, your worst-case scenario is getting stiffed, meaning you get $0 back. Her failure to repay you will certainly end your friendship, but at least your damages are capped at $2,000.

Suppose, instead of a request for a loan, your friend asks you to be a co-signer on a $20,000 auto loan. In this scenario, your exposure could be much, much worse. As a co-debtor, if she fails to make the car payments, you are responsible to pony up. As the co-signer, you are equally responsible for the entire debt as though you took the debt out on your own—but you do not get the benefit of driving or selling the car.

If your friend fails to make the car payments, the car will eventually be repossessed. After it is repossessed, it will be sold at auction for significantly less than it is worth. You will then be responsible for the deficiency between the loan balance and the auction sales price, penalties, interest, and late fees. If the repossessed car sells at auction for $13,000 and the balance of the loan is $19,000, you are responsible for the $6,000 deficiency, plus the fees and interest charged by the lender under the terms of the car loan, which will assuredly be thousands more. In this scenario, the one decision to be a co-signer could cost you thousands and thousands of dollars.

Besides automobile loans, cosigners are commonly seen on student loans. As a co-signer for a student loan, your liability could be tens of thousands of dollars. Your loved one may come to you with a desire to enter a new field with the hope of starting a new career as they enter the next chapter of their life. Again, **do not co-sign**. If you are still unclear on this point, consider your potential liability. If your loved one drops out of the program or fails to pay, you are responsible for 100% of the student loan. Your liability could be huge and derail your own journey toward financial success.

"Powdered Butt Syndrome"

There has been a trend of people at or near retirement age getting divorced. As such, you may find yourself as an adult being a confidant in your mother or father's post-separation financial recovery. If you are in such a position, your attempts at giving advice may be hampered by *powdered butt syndrome*.[30] This is the unscientific phrase to describe parents who are unable to take any sort of advice, financial or otherwise, from someone whose diaper they changed decades ago. This may perfectly describe your parent when you try to guide them on anything other than helping them navigate their electronic devices.

Ignoring the fact that their child has matured into an educated and kind-hearted adult, a parent may be unwilling or unable to listen to anything the child has to say about money due to the historical nature of the relationship. In such a situation,

---

30. While the origin of the phrase itself is unclear, Dave Ramsey has published a significant amount of content on this phenomenon.

take any resistance with a grain of salt. One way to deal with this is to find a family member or friend of theirs who can provide the same counsel but without the relational hindrance. It is most effective if the other person is held in high regard by your parent for their financial acumen, and this neutral party is willing to give the same guidance as you to steer your parent in the right direction.

While there is no creative descriptor for siblings or other family members who may rebuff advice, this same type of resistance may occur because of the very nature of your relationship. Siblings who were once competitive, for instance, might have an inherent roadblock that prevents meaningful discussions because of the divorcee's embarrassment, pride, or unwillingness to show weakness.

It is hard to overcome deep-rooted emotions in situations when longstanding relationships are involved, and I do not have a clear answer for you on how to deal with this. The best you can hope for in this situation is to keep the lines of communication open and respect their wishes.

Lead by example.

Helping your loved one walk the post-divorce journey to financial recovery does not require you to give money—just your time, compassion, encouragement, and honesty. If you are going to have in-depth conversations with them about their spending, saving, and overall financial health, you must be prepared to talk about your spending, saving, and relationship with money—but your actions are just as important as your words.

> *Setting an example is not the main means of influencing others; it is the only means.*
>
> **– Albert Einstein**

If you have never crafted a budget of your own, now is the time to learn to do so. You will be in a much more relatable position to the person you are trying to help because you will be practicing what you preach. If you have no idea where you are spending your own money, then you will not be able to offer much in terms of helpful advice or counsel when issues arise for those new to budgeting, including overspending on categories, failing to budget for certain expenses and the initial emotional drag that comes with this sweeping change in personal money management.

When I sit down with someone for the first time to help them take control of their finances, after learning about the income and debts, the next logical conversation is about budgeting. Almost always, those who have out-of-control finances live without a budget. For their behavior to change, they must first figure out where their money is going instead of wondering where it went (as the great John Maxwell famously teaches). Nevertheless, transitioning from a spendthrift lifestyle to one that requires premeditated diligence is never easy. Those new to budgeting frequently underestimate what they spend on restaurants, groceries, and fuel, as well as daily vices. Just like most everything else in life, there is a learning curve to budgeting.

If you have never lived on a budget and choose not to as you try to help your loved one in their financial recovery journey, your input and advice will be of limited value. You simply will not be in a position to talk about any challenge of adjusting to living on a budget or the struggles that accompany the adjustment from the unrestrained lifestyle. Creating a budget and adhering to it is tough, especially at the outset. It takes several months to get used to crafting the budget, making the necessary adjustments to each category, and incorporating things that have been overlooked. It also takes time to stop feeling like the budget is controlling you, like a parent controlling the behavior of their child.

The best advice I can offer if you want to help your loved one through this is to get on a budget yourself and stick to it. Then you will be able to share your struggles, explain the behavior changes you've experienced, and provide advice that you have learned during your journey. It will be easier for you to connect with the person you are trying to help, and you can be the accountability partner that is often needed for first-time budgeters.

If you have lived on a budget in your household for months or years, you are already going to have a wealth of knowledge and thus, be in a position to offer valuable advice, success stories, and struggles you have faced in your journey. Do not hesitate to acknowledge the difficulties you experienced those first few months when you transitioned to living on a budget because your personal experiences of those times are of tremendous value to someone just starting.

Part of leading by example is sharing your lowlights as well. Do not be afraid to share your blooper reel. Talk about the times you have been ripped off, regrettably succumbed to temptation, made impulse purchases you still feel angry about, and engaged in retail therapy. Talk openly about the things you wish you could say to the younger version of yourself. This will create an open dialogue and build trust with the person you are trying to help. It also allows you to be approachable and not judgmental when your loved one makes a mistake, engages in retail therapy, or blows the budget in a moment of weakness—any of which are likely to occur during their journey.

It is never too late to help.

Regardless of where your loved one is in their post-divorce recovery process—meaning whether their divorce was finalized ten days ago or ten years ago—it is never too late to offer a helping hand. It is amazing how much can be discussed over a cup of coffee, a drink at your local tavern, or a meal while dining out, especially when you are the one offering to pay. If a significant amount of time has passed since you last spoke, it may be appropriate to apologize for letting the time slip away. It is okay to admit that you could have been more present for them earlier in the process because your goal is to clear the air. Do not be afraid to say that the reason you asked them out for coffee was that you were thinking about them and wanted to see how things were going. You may be the first person to have asked them about their situation in months.

Respect boundaries and recognize when your assistance is unwanted.

One of the books I frequently recommend (including in Part I of this book) to clients is *Boundaries: When to Say Yes, How to Say No to Take Control of Your Life* by Dr. Henry Cloud and Dr. John Townsend. It does a fantastic job of teaching the reader to recognize how people encroach on our boundaries, the impact boundary-violators and no-boundary relationships have on us, and methods to establish boundaries in all aspects of our lives.

As a member of the support network of someone who has endured a divorce, you must respect the boundaries of your loved one. They may not be ready to talk about finances or any other personal topic with you, despite your readiness and eagerness to help. You may see them make mistake after mistake with money, leading you to wonder, *"should I say something or should I keep my mouth shut?"*

While I do not have all the answers for you, I do know that relationships can be ruined if the situation is handled incorrectly and your loved one's boundaries aren't respected. You should never respond to a rebuke of your attempts to help with hostility or anger because that is the quickest way to tank your relationship. Even if you are a self-made multimillionaire and professional financial advisor, if your loved one doesn't want your advice or help, there is nothing you can do to change that. Keep the door open by saying things like, *"if you ever want me to help you with your budget, I'm happy to do so"* or *"I am always available if you ever want to talk about anything."* Despite your efforts, your advice still may never be sought, welcomed, or needed.

Even if your offers to help are declined, do not close the door completely. Your loved one is in recovery mode, after all, and every divorcee recovers from such an impactful, life-changing event at their own speed. The emotional recovery may take years, and the financial recovery may not be a priority until the emotional scars have healed. Thus, an offer to accompany your loved one on their journey toward a financial recovery made shortly after the divorce is finalized may not be appreciated until several years have passed.

---

*God, grant me the serenity to accept
the things I cannot change,
the courage to change the things I can,
and the wisdom to know the difference*

- The Serenity Prayer

Bless your heart if you are reading this because you want to help someone you care about get their financial life together following their divorce. I truly wish you the best because you are in an unenviable and sometimes agonizing position. I hope that this book has given you ideas, guidance, and inspiration as you go forward in your role as a confidant, accountability partner, and advocate for someone who clearly means a lot to you.

The unfortunate caveat to everything said in here is similar to what I would say if you wanted to help someone quit smoking or lose weight: success hinges upon the behavior and decisions made by the person you wish to help. My spouse may want me to lose a few pounds, but all of her hoping and praying that I lose weight is not going to result in any change to my weight unless I want it for myself. You may want your best friend to quit smoking, but there is nothing you can do to change their behavior, regardless of the extent of your efforts. Your loved one's personal finances are no different.

Despite this, I encourage you never to give up your willingness and eagerness to be there for your loved one when it comes to their finances. Eventually, something in their life will give them a wake-up call. A lost job, missed car payment, declined credit card, or a sudden overwhelming feeling of panic are all capable of inspiring a change of behavior. If you consistently show through your words and actions that you are there and willing to help, I suspect that at some point, your loved one will seek out advice, and you will be fully ready at that time to answer the call for help.

Afterword

I wrote this book because I want to help you in any way I can. You face an arduous journey under harsh circumstances. It is my sincere hope that you can apply the concepts that you've learned in this book to your own life and that the months and years ahead will be better as a result.

This book is meant to get you started on your way, but it cannot and should not be the end of your financial education. Refer to Appendix A for a list of the books and resources I have recommended and discussed. Since there are so many of them, I listed them in order of priority. If you are only going to read two or three more books, choose from the ones at the top of the list. While there are countless other personal finance books that I have read, enjoyed, and are worth your time, you can find yourself getting conflicting advice depending on the author and their viewpoint of debt. As such, until your journey is well underway and the lessons taught by the endorsed authors are well entrenched in your mind, stick to the content produced by the authors on Appendix A. They are all consistent with one another, and each has enough content in written, audio, and visual formats I doubt you will have time to consume it all.

Throughout this book, I heavily advocate the teachings of Dave Ramsey for getting out of debt and the complementary teachings of Jack Bogle and J.L. Collins for investing and wealth building. I am not compensated at all for these recommendations. I just have the utmost respect for their teachings, books, and overall devotion to helping others like you and me. Most importantly, what they teach works.

I am debt-free because Dave Ramsey showed me the way. My wife and I certainly had to do all of the hard work, but I am convinced that we would still have debts in our lives without his guidance. The impact that his get-out-of-debt methodology has had for me and my family has been so great that I feel compelled to share it with those who are looking for direction. My sentiments are shared by millions of people who have also freed themselves from the shackles of debt thanks to his plan.

Since this journey can be long and because you will inevitably encounter rough spots along the way, questions and predicaments will come up that are not answered or explained in the preceding pages. This is one of the main reasons I have total comfort telling you to follow Ramsey's guidance. He and his team have created digital content to answer almost every question imaginable about personal finance. There are videos on YouTube, articles on *DaveRamsey.com*, podcasts, and more—all intended to provide you with guidance and in-depth answers, and all free of charge. Should any questions come up about a specific problem or issue, an excellent place to start is to type "Dave Ramsey" and your question into Google. I would bet good money that you find the answer in a matter of seconds. To leave you without a way to continue your education and find answers to your questions would be irresponsible on my part. Therefore, I am confident that Ramsey and his team will continually provide you with trustworthy guidance and advice that I would echo if you were to ask me directly.

Bogle and Collins carry the torch for both investing and the greater mission of achieving financial independence. You are in good hands if you follow their teachings, and financial freedom is an attainable goal for you if you are dedicated to your mission. Collins' book covers literally every stage you can encounter as you work towards total financial freedom, so it is good to keep a copy around as a reference as you approach later ages and encounter nuanced situations. Collins also has an active website and blog that is also worth your time, which can be found at *JLCollinsNH.com*.

Personal finance is personal, so you must decide your comfort level when it comes to investing. If you prefer that an advisor help you make investing decisions, use an advisor. If you prefer to do it on your own, go for it. Just avoid the "paralysis by analysis" approach of doing nothing because you feel too overwhelmed by the situation. If you save and invest nothing for your retirement, you will end up with nothing at retirement.

I follow the guidance of the authors I recommend in this book. I have read countless others, but there is no doubt in my mind that collectively, Ramsey, Bogle, and Collins offer the most direct, understandable, and comprehensive approach to lead you to the promised land of financial independence. Follow their advice, as well as the guidance I have given you about how to avoid devastating divorcee-susceptible mistakes, and you will achieve much more than just a financial recovery—you will attain true financial freedom.

Finally, feel free to contact me through my website, *MikeJurek.com*, and let me know how your journey is going. Share your successes and slip-ups. If you need additional guidance, I will do my best to help. I want to see you succeed in your financial recovery just as much as you do, and I look forward to celebrating the small and large victories with you along the way.

Time to get to work!

> *Be bold and mighty forces will come to your aid.*
>
> **- Basil King**

Acknowledgments

To my beautiful wife, thank you for being so supportive of all of the nights and weekends I spent writing this book. Your boundless love and constant encouragement fuel me in so many ways.

To my precious daughter who was born half way into my writing of this book, thank you for all of the spontaneous and very early morning wake-up calls that inspired me to tackle the blank page instead of going back to sleep.

To my mom and dad, sister, and all of my family, thanks for your endless support of all of my endeavors.

Dave Warren—I lost count of the number of drafts you proofread for me over the last two years. I cannot thank you enough for your help in transforming this from an idea to an outline, and from an outline into this book. Above and beyond, my friend.

Steve Swick, without your initial support and brainstorming, this book does not exist.

To Adam Pratt, thank you for helping me with the final edit with this project, and generally for your advice and wisdom over the last 19 years.

Robb Stokar, Adam Mele, David Zitt, and Teelin Henderson—I talk a lot in this book about the value of a good support network. You, gentlemen, are the best support network one could ask for. The number of hours you collectively spent listening to me talk about this book warrants at least one drink for each of you, on me, during happy hour, domestics only.

To my law partners and friends at Dungan & LeFevre in Troy, Ohio—I am proud to work with such a dedicated and skilled group of attorneys. Thanks again for the support.

Finally, to all of my mentors, I can trace my greatest successes back to those of you who took the time to provide me with guidance and direction at various points in my life. The older I get, the more I realize how impactful mentors have been in my life. This seems like as good of a time as any to say thanks.

Appendix A—Recommended Books

Below are the ten books I strongly recommend as follow-up reading, in the order of priorty:

Author(s)	Title
Dave Ramsey	*The Total Money Makeover: A Proven Plan for Financial Fitness*
John C. Bogle	*The Little Book of Common Sense Investing: The Only Way to Guarantee Your Fair Share of Stock Market Returns*
J.L. Collins	*The Simple Path to Wealth: Your Roadmap to Financial Independence and a Rich, Free Life*
Dr. Thomas Stanley & Dr. William Danko	*The Millionaire Next Door: The Surprising Secrets of America's Wealthy*
Dr. Henry Cloud & Dr. John Townsend	*Boundaries: When to Say Yes, How to Say No to Take Control of Your Life*
Katie McKenna	*How to Get Run Over by a Truck*
Rachel Cruze	*Love Your Life Not Theirs: 7 Money Habits for Living the Life You Want*
Chris Hogan	*Retire Inspired: It's Not an Age, It's a Financial Number*
Dave Ramsey	*EntreLeadership: 20 Years of Practical Business Wisdom from the Trenches*
Christy Wright	*Business Boutique: A Woman's Guide for Making Money Doing What She Loves*

Printed in Great Britain
by Amazon

23507305R00136